Miss Bridges

The brides of Kensington

Miss Bridges

The brides of Kensington

ISBN/EAN: 9783741191725

Manufactured in Europe, USA, Canada, Australia, Japa

Cover: Foto ©Andreas Hilbeck / pixelio.de

Manufactured and distributed by brebook publishing software (www.brebook.com)

Miss Bridges

The brides of Kensington

THE BRIDES OF KENSINGTON.

CHAPTER I.

It was sunset on the Lake of Geneva. Mont Blanc was ablaze with glory. Colours which seemed too bright for earth, and which varied every moment, like the hues of a kaleidoscope, transfigured the scene, till it became paradisiacal, and you almost expected that the golden gates would open and admit you into the presence of angels.

An English family group was gathered in the balcony of the Clarence Hotel. It contained first of all a lady, the summer of whose life was verging on the autumnal. Lady Sarah Mowbray was a magnificent woman, tall and majestic, with fine blue eyes, and hair which had once been black as the raven's wing. At first sight her presence awed you, but the moment that you heard her kindly voice, and felt the charm of her perfect manner, you began to love her. Her eldest daughter, Margaret, was the image of herself, only that her eyes were dark, and her figure had the sylph-like proportions of early womanhood. Her hair was of a rich brown, with golden lights in it when it caught the sun, and a cluster of heavy curls fell behind from a tortoise-shell comb. Her sister, Guendolen, was short and plump, with light hazel eyes and hair to match. She wore a wavy fringe over her forehead, which imparted a certain child-like grace to a countenance which would have otherwise startled you by its premature astuteness.

A gentleman was in attendance, who claimed kinship with these fair ladies. Being the orphan son of a favourite cousin, St. John Munro had always been treated by Lady Sarah with the utmost kindness; and he had been accustomed in his youth to spend his holidays at Lancaster Court, which was a few miles from London.

'How glorious!' exclaimed Margaret, turning to her mother, while her eyes were suffused with tears. 'I wish Emily was here; I cannot think what makes her so late.'

'Haven't you enough beauty to satisfy even you for the present?' asked St. John, withdrawing his eyes from the splendid view to fix them on the girl whom he addressed.

'I always like to have those whom I most love to share my enjoyment,' she replied.

A sort of shadow crossed the marble brow of St. John, his eye flashed a glance of reproach at his cousin, and he remarked sarcastically:

'I always dislike the superlative degree.'

'Are you jealous of Emily before you have seen her?' mischievously inquired Guendolen.

"'Like Alexander I would reign,
And I would reign alone,'"

was the playful retort of St. John, as his eye again rested with a look of conscious power on the now blushing Margaret.

At this moment the door opened and the waiter announced—'Lord and Miss Fitzalan.'

The first of these visitors was a man of stately presence, many years older than his beautiful sister, around whom the ladies gathered with affectionate caresses.

'What has made you so late?' inquired the hostess, as she took the arm of her newly arrived guest, and led the way to the supper-room.

'To tell you the truth,' he replied, 'I had a curiosity to hear the Roman Catholic Bishop preach at your cathedral. He is certainly a wonderful man. My little sister here wants to make his acquaintance.'

'She can easily do that,' said Lady Sarah. 'We expect the honour of his presence here to-morrow evening, to meet a few friends, and you must both come.'

The invitation was accepted with a beaming look of gratitude from Emily's blue eyes, which was not lost on the observant St. John.

Whoever has listened to the thrilling eloquence of Monseigneur Mermillod, will be able to understand the effect which his discourse, delivered with the most glowing unction, produced upon the enthusiastic mind of Miss Fitzalan. She had been brought up, like her brother, in the cold philosophy of Unitarianism. Her intellect had been highly cultivated, but the religious impulses of

her ardent nature had never found a vent. On
this particular Sunday evening, Monseigneur
Mermillod had chosen for his subject—The
Mystery of the Adorable Trinity. It was like the
aurora of a new life to Emily. The vision of the
Godhead flashed upon her soul with a splendour
that was almost intolerable. The eternal genera-
tion of the Most High God, ' still begetting, still
begotten, still His own perfections seeing,' subdued her intelligence and captivated her heart.
But her emotion was so deep, that not even to
Adrian, her beloved, her adored brother, could
she unbosom herself as yet, even if she could
have expected sympathy, which was very far
from being the case. His lordship's anti-Catholic
prejudices were too notorious.

CHAPTER II.

It was a happy party that assembled at the
Clarence Hotel on the following evening. There
were several visitors, and a murmur of suppressed
admiration went round the room when Miss
Fitzalan entered on the arm of her brother. She
was simply attired in white tarlatane, and her
tresses of pale gold were artistically braided.
Her countenance was so full of soul that it could
not fail to interest the most ordinary spectator.
When the Bishop of Geneva was announced a
flush of the deepest carnation suffused her cheek.
Margaret was standing next to her, and said :

'Monseigneur, permit me to present my special friend, Miss Fitzalan.'

He took her hand with one of his beaming smiles, and expressed his pleasure at making her acquaintance. He was quite the life of the party. Lord Fitzalan, whose powers of conversation were usually great, was more than commonly silent. Towards the close of the evening the young people strolled into the garden. Emily alone remained in the drawing-room. It happened that the Bishop was particularly interested in looking over some choice illuminations which Lady Sarah had just completed. A servant entered on some particular errand to the hostess, who, with a graceful apology, requested Miss Fitzalan to take her place in entertaining her Right Reverend guest until her return. Emily was generally distinguished for the perfect ease of her manner in society, but on this occasion it seemed to desert her; she became flushed, and then pale as death, while the taper fingers of her beautiful hands unconsciously pulled to pieces the bouquet which adorned her corsage. Monseigneur Mermillod saw her embarrassment, and that it proceeded from something deeper than shyness. He seemed to be observing the picture before him, and remarked, without looking at her:

'Lady Sarah, without intending it, has given to this Madonna the features and the expression of Miss Mowbray.'

'Yes,' said Emily, 'it is true;' then after a pause she added, 'That notion of a Divine maternity seems to be a source of great consolation to Catholics.'

'It is a tie for which every human heart has a yearning,' said the Bishop.

'Do you know,' said the young lady, 'that I went to hear your sermon last night, and it opened a new world to me?'

The eye of the Bishop now met hers, with a look of bright intelligence; and Emily continued, without any further trace of agitation:

'I mean a new world of thought and inquiry. Pardon me if, after so short an acquaintance, I venture to remark that there are questions which I should like to ask you.'

'I am always at the service of any inquirer after truth, my child. I shall be at home all the afternoon to-morrow. Are you making a long stay at Geneva?'

'My brother goes away in a few days, but I am to remain here on a visit to the Mowbrays for some weeks after his departure.'

'I am glad to hear it,' said the Bishop.

At this moment others of the party joined them, and the conversation became general.

On the following morning Miss Fitzalan had a long conversation alone with Margaret, and confided to her the earnest wish that she felt to see more of the eloquent preacher. Her friend was only too glad to co-operate with her, and arranged with her mother's cognizance to take her to the Bishop's house for an interview.

Monseigneur's mind, rapid as lightning and clear as crystal, took in all her difficulties, and dissipated them. He promised to pray for her, and appointed a time for their next conversation.

When Emily joined her brother at his own

hotel, in the evening, she told him candidly what had taken place; but she was not prepared for the tempest of passion which her statement evoked.

'Do you dare tell me,' he exclaimed, 'that this fascinating prelate is tampering with you? Let him beware!'

'I thought you admired his eloquence on Sunday,' said his sister.

'So I did, as I might admire the talent of Lucifer. Listen to me, Emily! It would shake my very soul to its foundations if you were to become a Roman Catholic!'

'Then why did you allow me to be so intimate with the Mowbrays when we were in England?'

'Because I admire the talents and the elegance of Lady Sarah and her daughters. You could not have better associates as far as all that goes; but I never dreamed of your being caught in that web of superstition.'

'Still you do not like them the less for being Catholics,' suggested the girl.

'Their ancestors were Catholics before them; they could not help themselves.'

'I beg your pardon—Lady Sarah was a convert.'

'One can hardly blame a young and beautiful girl, as I have heard she was, for being overpersuaded by the sophistries of such a man as Colonel Mowbray. But you, with your splendid education and your fine mind, it is a different thing.'

'I don't think that my intellect, however your affection may overrate it, can be supposed to rank higher than Margaret Mowbray's,' and the young lady lifted her clear, grey eyes, with a decidedly mischievous expression to those of her brother.

'Margaret—Miss Mowbray, I mean—is a very superior girl,' replied Lord Fitzalan, while a hot flush mounted to his brow; 'but understand, Emily, once for all, I forbid you to have anything further to do with this Monseigneur! Do you hear me?'

'Yes; I hear you,' said Emily, coming up and throwing her soft arms round his neck.

She had hitherto been so submissive to his wishes, that the idea did not cross his mind that she could possibly dispute or evade his will now that he had distinctly announced it, nor did she dare to do so openly; but she resolved that Miss Mowbray should explain to the Bishop that she must defer the privilege of another interview until after her brother's departure.

Emily was extremely gentle in manner; there was an indescribable refinement about her which came from the heart's core, and constituted her principal charm. But she possessed great strength of character under that soft alluring exterior. On this occasion she certainly was not quite straightforward with her brother. We do not pretend that she was perfect—far otherwise. Her nature was dreamy and poetical, her instincts were fastidious. She had plenty of kindly and benevolent impulses, arising from a fund of native generosity; but she was often culpably indolent, though capable of energy. Hitherto she had passed through her short life gracefully, but without an object. Her principal aim had been to please her brother, to whom she was tenderly devoted; and now the hitherto placid waters of her mind were beginning to be disturbed by a violent conflict.

After the last conversation that we have recorded, she went to her room, and, having dismissed her maid, sat at the window, which commanded a quiet view and could not be overlooked. It did not occur to her what a pretty picture she made in her snowy drapery, with her hair falling loose in a golden cloud. The moon was shining over the lake, and the whole world seemed to be etherealized. But a vision of more than mortal beauty was at that moment filling the mind of Miss Fitzalan. It was the thought of God! She had known Him hitherto as a mere abstraction, and now she was beginning to learn some of His perfections from the lips of one of His devoted servants.

'Oh! I could do anything for such a God— I could suffer anything for such a Redeemer!' she thought. 'And yet it will be dreadful to displease Adrian. He looked as if his very love for me would change if I crossed him in this matter. Could I live without him—without his affection? I doubt it. At least, I can die, and then he will break his heart. Thou Who hast made me, have mercy on me!'

All night long she pondered and prayed, and it was not till the morning was advanced that she threw herself on her couch for a few hours' rest.

CHAPTER III.

ST. JOHN and Margaret had walked together that same evening.

'What have you been doing since dinner?' interrogated the former.

'I have been to church,' replied his cousin.

'And somewhere else,' he pursued.

'Yes; I went to the Bishop's house,' and she lifted her blue eyes to his with a steady ingenuous expression, which implied, 'I have told you all I mean to, and I shall say no more.'

'Now, Margaret,' said he, 'let me give you a warning. I know who was with you, and I think it will be dishonourable if you aid and abet Miss Fitzalan in any scheme that would incur her brother's disapproval.'

'You must permit me,' she replied with dignity, 'to be the judge of what is honourable in any case in which my friends are concerned.'

'Is Adrian to be made acquainted with the event of this afternoon?'

'Certainly,' replied the young lady; 'but you will oblige me by not alluding to the subject to anyone. Emily does not wish to have attention drawn to her proceedings.'

'"But once beguiled, and ever more beguiling,"' he muttered to himself.

'St. John, you have no right to apply that term in the present case.'

'How long have you known Miss Fitzalan?' he asked, somewhat irrelevantly.

'For several years,' she replied; 'though it

has always happened that you were at college or abroad when she was in our neighbourhood. Is she not lovely ?'

'Rather!' he replied, with a peculiar expression. 'She is absolutely under the guardianship of this brother, I understand. Adrian is a splendid fellow, and good company; but I fancy you might get yourself into a scrape if you crossed his wishes. It would be hardly safe to make an enemy of that man. I have seen a demon in his eye now and then!'

'St John, you are always cautious and worldly wise. As for me, I rather enjoy running a risk, and driving along the edge of a precipice—just managing not to topple over.'

And she laughed saucily, throwing in his face a handful of daisies which she had gathered.

He looked at her with a fonder admiration than she had ever seen in his eyes before. He took both her hands in his, flower-soiled as they were, and gloveless—and said, with unusual earnestness:

'Margaret, my pearl of cousins, promise me that you will not let any secret or mystery come between you and me.'

The unaccustomed pathos in his voice moved her, but she hated coquetry. She loved him as a brother, and had hitherto treated him with a sister's playful and innocent freedom. She had never till this moment dreamed that he regarded her in any other light. But the truth now dawned upon her. She shook herself free, and said: 'Let go, you naughty boy. I shall promise nothing of the kind.'

St. John was deeply mortified, for he had made rather too sure of his ground.

'You are a pretty girl, and a plucky girl!' he exclaimed; 'but your ladyship will have to come down a peg or two one of these fine days, I expect. Here comes Guendolen to welcome us home,' he added.

The second Miss Mowbray had a touch of green in her eyes. Nevertheless they were fine eyes, and looked well under the curly fringe, which was not long enough to take away the expression from her fair and well-formed forehead. A certain anxiety was disturbing her mind; but she had a good deal of self-control, and it was with her most charming manner that she accosted her relatives.

'I have heard from Sophy,' she said, 'and she tells me great news. She is going to be a nun; Myrtle Cottage is to be shut up. What do you think of that?'

'That she will never stay,' said St. John.

'I am surprised,' said Margaret; 'but I am glad to hear it.'

'Because it will take her out of my way, n'est-ce pas?' asked Guendolen, with a jealous glance at her sister.

'You are quite right, dear,' said Margaret candidly, 'I can't bear the woman, and I dislike the influence which she is getting over you. Pardon me, if I speak unkindly of your friend.'

'I quite acknowledge,' said Guendolen, 'that there is a spice of the devil in her, but she is a darling all the same, and you can't deny that she is handsome, can you, St. John?'

'I hate her,' replied that gentleman, most ungallantly, 'and I believe she returns the compliment.'

He shot an inquiring glance at his younger cousin, who, however, looked imperturbable and remarked:

'Oh, the vanity of men! They are always dying to know what a woman thinks of them! But say no more, for here comes mamma.'

'And her dutiful daughter,' added St. John, 'has divers little secret corners in her heart which she fancies are hidden from the maternal eye.'

He said this somewhat bitterly, for he was out of humour, and his words jarred on Guendolen. The tears welled in her eyes, and Margaret exclaimed:

'Don't tease her, St. John; you are always at that game.'

'Don't cry, there's a dear!' said the young man, lifting her hand to his lips, for he really liked her. 'Am I forgiven?'

'Too easily, perhaps,' said the girl, with her sweetest smile and her prettiest air.

When she went to her room that night, she fell into a sort of waking dream.

'He would love me,' she said to herself, 'if it were not for that queenly sister of mine. If we could only get her engaged to Lord Fitzalan, it would all be right. But if Margaret puts herself out in that quarter, and she is capable of any madness where her enthusiasm is concerned, there is no answering for the consequences. I can't think how she can take St. John's attentions so calmly. She obeys him, too, in many things. Perhaps that is because he taught her Latin, and she looks up to him intellectually. It is a bad thing for a man to teach a girl, unless he is an old grey-beard. I have a great mind to learn something from him. Shall I ask him to give me lessons in Euclid? I should get on better than most boys. But then he is so sharp, he would twig my object. What a relief it is to think a little slang, as mamma is so particular about our conversation! One thing I like in Sophy is, she is so lawless; and there is so much style about her that she can do things that no one else could without being vulgar. I can see that Emily is already on the Bishop's hook. I saw it the first evening they came, before she had spoken to him. That girl is awfully reserved in her speech to me, but she has a tell-tale countenance which constantly betrays her. And now she will be getting up some red-hot piety which will put her brother in a blaze, and take off his thoughts from courtship. What fools people are! But it will fade my roses if I sit up longer; and the Swiss air has made me look remarkably pretty of late. I wish my figure was as good as my face. I cannot compete with Margaret there.'

Hereupon she got up from her sofa, and prepared for her night's rest.

By the end of the week Lord Fitzalan had commenced his journey to England, leaving his sister under the kind chaperonage of Lady Sarah. Miss Fitzalan was so devoted to her brother that she could not part from him, even for a few weeks, without feeling it deeply. The affection was equally strong on his side.

'You will take care of my treasure, Lady Sarah,' said the young man gallantly; 'and make her like yourself in all things save one.'

'I admit no exceptions,' said her ladyship. 'Emily will be dearer to me than I can say. But you must take the consequences of the peril which you expose her to. I make no false pretences.'

There was a charm to him in the courage as well as in the sweetness with which she spoke.

'Emily knows my mind,' he remarked; 'and I think that is enough.'

He kissed his sister's cheek, which was pale as marble, and made his adieus.

When he was out of sight, Miss Fitzalan attempted to cross the hall, wishing to be alone in her room. But her hostess, who saw that she was almost fainting from the violence of suppressed emotion, gently drew her away into her own boudoir, placed her on a sofa, and made her take a glass of wine.

'My own dear child,' she said, 'it will not be many weeks before you will rejoin your brother, and in the meantime I want you to enjoy yourself.'

'I dread to think that this is the foreshadowing of a longer separation,' said the girl, laying her head with a pretty dependent air against the sympathizing bosom of her faithful friend.

Lady Sarah understood her so well that she asked no questions, but gave her a kiss, took up her work, and permitted her *protégée* to enjoy the relief of quiet thought. After an interval, Emily spoke:

'I think you have bewitched my brother, Lady Sarah. I can't think what can possess him, with his prejudices, to trust me to you. He admires you to such a degree——'

'Hush, little flatterer! you have said quite enough;' and a beautiful white hand, soft as velvet, was laid on Emily's lips.

But the young lady caught it with a saucy grace, and continued:

'Adrian seems to forget that I have a right to be fascinated by you as well as himself. But I hope you will keep your influence over him, dear Lady Sarah; promise me that you will. Don't throw it aside out of any false humility.'

'I am quite aware,' said the elder lady, 'that influence, like every other good gift, should be used for the glory of Almighty God. And you need not fear that I shall neglect any opportunity of improving any little power I may possess over your brother's mind. If anything in the future should make him withdraw his confidence from me, I shall deeply regret it.'

'I do not believe it will,' said Emily. 'He thinks that you have a right to be a Catholic, because Colonel Mowbray is of the ancient faith. But I must not forget that I have no time to lose. Dear Lady Sarah, would you mind sending a note from me to the Bishop, requesting the favour of an interview?'

'It shall be done at once, darling.'

'And I don't wish anyone except Margaret to know.'

'Very well. I will manage it.'

Accordingly, Lady Sarah enclosed Miss Fitzalan's

note in one of her own, and desired her young people to profit by the beauty of the evening, and take a walk. They had not long left the hotel when Monseigneur arrived, and had a long conversation with Emily. Lady Sarah threw open the door of her own morning-room, which communicated with the saloon, and occupied herself there, in order to leave her guests free, and yet to take off the appearance of a *téte-à-téte*. Miss Fitzalan had a considerable acquaintance with the doctrines of the Catholic religion, from her general reading, which had been varied and extensive from her childhood upwards; and she showed a marvellous facility in grasping the truths which were now unfolded to her. She was particularly attracted by the dogma of the Real Presence; to have our God so near to us—upon our altars, in our hearts—the idea was fraught with the highest joy to Emily. Before they parted, she inquired:

'How soon will you permit me to be a Catholic, Monseigneur?'

'Are you prepared to admit the authority of the Church as the depositary and exponent of all Truth?'

'Indeed I am,' she replied.

'I see that you are sufficiently informed as to the details of our belief. After a few more instructions as to the mode of preparing for the sacraments, I shall be able to receive your abjuration. But if possible, I should like your brother to be made acquainted with your intentions. It is always so much better to be candid and straightforward.'

'I feel certain,' she replied, 'that my brother would exert his authority as my guardian to prevent my being a Catholic. I am only twenty years of age, and he would take me away at once from my kind friends. At present he feels secure that I shall not cross his wishes after the strong things which he said before his departure.'

'And you did not undeceive him?' said the Bishop.

'No; I kept silence, and let him go away under his mistake.'

'That alters the case: if an avowal to your natural guardian would absolutely prevent your conversion, I cannot counsel you to make it. I will receive you into the Church next week.'

'Thank God!' said Emily; 'I feel that I can bear anything now. But I shall have to keep my religion a secret until I am of age.'

'You must do the best you can, dear child. May God bless you.'

Monseigneur Mermillod had left the Clarence Hotel before the walking-party returned.

St. John had been somewhat abstracted during the walk with his cousins. He would have preferred their all remaining at home, so that he might keep a watch over Emily, who interested him excessively. Still, he would not have foregone the pleasure of Margaret's society for any consideration. He was, in fact, deeply attached to her; and he made sure, perhaps a little too sure, that his affection was returned. It was flattering to his vanity that so brilliant a girl should defer to him on many points, as she certainly did. There was a great deal of intellectual sympathy between them, though it was a source of deep regret to Miss Mowbray that her cousin, though nominally a Catholic, cared little for religion. He had a considerable spice of curiosity for a man. He made his way straight to the sofa where Miss Fitzalan was sitting, and, bending over her in a graceful elder-brotherly sort of way, began questioning her as to how she had spent the evening. Of course he soon elicited the name of her visitor, and that she had not seen him alone; but beyond that Emily was impenetrable.

The event of her reception into the true fold of Christ, which took place the following week, together with the two great sacraments of First Communion and Confirmation, was all managed with such consummate tact by Lady Sarah, that not a creature in the hotel knew anything about it, excepting Miss Mowbray, who stood by her friend in the capacity of bridesmaid, with a lighted candle and a bouquet of white flowers, when Emily approached the altar to receive the Holy Eucharist. St. John and Guendolen had watched and spied, but all to no purpose. When Sunday came they wondered where she would go. Emily remained at home. They little thought that she had risen at a very early hour when they were fast asleep, and assisted at the sacrifice of the Mass at the old church, which was a long way off, and remote from observation.

Miss Fitzalan was profoundly happy. She had found all she wanted in the bosom of the Spouse of Christ. Her soul reposed in a sense of supernatural fulness. She felt that she could leave the future, with all its anxieties, in the hands of an Almighty Father.

Two months rolled away in this blissful peace. Now and then she had accompanied her hostess and the rest of the family to High Mass at the Cathedral on a Sunday, but not often enough to be taken as evidence of conversion. At last the time came when they had all arranged to return to England. It was a pleasant October evening when they found themselves re-united at Lancaster Court. Lord Fitzalan was there to welcome them. Bright fires blazed in the reception-rooms. They were enjoying the refreshment of a high tea after their journey, and were in the midst of animated conversation, when the wheels of a carriage were heard driving over the gravel. 'Whoever can this be, at such a time of night?' was eagerly inquired. The gentlemen drew aside the heavy window curtains and looked out. But before they could arrive at any conclusion, the door opened; a lady entered, dressed in black silk, and heavily muffled up. She threw aside her veil, and words of astonishment burst from the party: 'Sophy!' 'Mrs. Vivian!' She bowed to Lady Sarah, and then fervently embraced Guendolen.

'My darling, what has happened?' was that young lady's exclamation. 'Have you left the Convent?'

'Yes; I have run away, a fortnight after taking the veil. You see, I am an obstreperous creature, and they pulled the cord too tight. I couldn't stand being boxed up.'

'I should think not,' said St. John, with one of

his cynical smiles. 'It would require a police force to keep you in order.'

The young widow coloured under the sarcasm.

'So you are not surprised that I took the law into my own hands, and set myself free?'

'I should have wondered if you had acted in a more rational manner.'

'I thought you always used to dislike convents; and I must say that you have become dreadfully rude.'

'When a lady asks my opinion about an escapade, she has no right to complain if it is an unflattering one.'

'St. John, I am ashamed of you!' remarked Guendolen.

'I advise you to retain and to cultivate that sentiment,' said her cousin, with a glance full of meaning: 'it is a desirable one for young ladies who are given to hero worship.'

Guendolen was blushing to the very roots of her hair, when Lord Fitzalan interposed:

'St. John, I must really protest against your bullying the fair sex in my presence.'

'My dear fellow, what's the good of having cousins if one can't speak one's mind to them?'

'St. John, you have gone too far; let me hear no more of this sort of thing,' said Lady Sarah, though she thought the snub might be useful to her younger daughter, who now commenced imploring her, in a low voice, to offer a night's hospitality to her friend. But Lady Sarah was firm in refusing to do this. 'No, my child,' she said, 'Mrs. Vivian has acted in a most disedifying way, by her own account, and it shall never be said that I sanction such unauthorized conduct.'

'But you cannot turn her out, mamma, at such an hour as this; her own house is shut up, as you know.'

Lady Sarah now turned to her unexpected visitor, and said calmly, but with great dignity:

'Mrs. Vivian, you must pardon my saying that I condemn your conduct in running away, as you call it, from a religious establishment. Nothing would have been easier than for you to have told your superiors that you wished to leave, and then they would have facilitated your doing so in a respectable way. I am sorry that under these circumstances I cannot offer you the hospitality of my home for the night. But if you will take some refreshment here, I will send a servant with you to the hotel, where you will have no difficulty in finding suitable accommodation.

Mrs. Vivian felt ready to sink into the earth under this just rebuke; but she had a good deal of brass in her composition. Guendolen whispered to her—' Never mind mamma; she is always high-flown. I should have acted just as you did, I dare say.'

Now it happened that Mrs. Vivian was excessively hungry, and the sight of the well-spread table was too great a temptation to be resisted. She, therefore, seated herself without further ceremony, and did justice to the repast.

These two young women had been at the same convent school, and had become extremely intimate while there. Lady Sarah had never liked the widow, but she had abstained from absolutely forbidding the acquaintance, and Miss Guendolen, if she was allowed an inch, always took an ell.

'That Mrs. Vivian is a fine woman,' remarked Lord Fitzalan to his sister, when they were alone in the carriage which was to take her to her own home. 'Do you know, I admire her pluck!'

'She has handsome eyes and a dashing manner,' said Emily. 'I saw that she was setting her cap at you.'

'And your manner was not encouraging—and she felt it too! You girls are dreadfully jealous and suspicious,' he added, with a laugh; 'but you may say or do anything you like to-night; I am so glad to have you back again!'

As they drove up to Stuart House, the servants who composed their comfortable but moderate establishment, were congregated in the hall to welcome their young mistress, who felt the warm delight of being at home again, even after such happy travels.

CHAPTER IV.

GUENDOLEN was closeted with Mrs. Vivian at the hotel the whole of the next morning. Their conversation had reference principally to the convent which that lady had fled from, and against which she had no substantial grievance to allege beyond having her will crossed. When they had talked this thoroughly over, Mrs. Vivian said:

'And now tell me all about the Honourable Emily. She has improved both in looks and in style since I saw her last; but there is something about her which I distrust. And the little minx did not take the trouble to veil her dislike of me.'

'I feel just as you do,' said Guendolen. 'There is a mystery which I cannot fathom; and she seems always on her guard against me. Mamma and Margaret are cracked about her, and I fancy they know something. I suspect she is a Catholic, and will not own it.'

'Thanks, *cara mia*, for that little clue. And St. John?' continued the widow, with a penetrating glance at her friend.

'I don't think he quite believes in her. He considers her very deep, and so she is. Her brother does not see through her.'

'I used to think that there was a friendly feeling between Mr. St. John Munro and Miss Guendolen Mowbray, when we all met at Brighton last year—all, I mean, except your sister.'

The bright colour rushed to the young lady's cheeks, but she answered calmly:

'St. John has the provoking quality of being able to worship two girls at the same time; I do not mean to imply that he is so dishonourable as to pay marked attentions to more than one: but he can feel an interest in two.'

'Then I would throw him over, and go in for the handsome lord!'

'Sophy, I am shocked at you. What would mamma say, if she heard you.'

'Of course she would say that I am a dreadful woman, and that young ladies should never think of such things—that they should grow up like beautiful violets in the shade, etc. Who is the other young lady besides yourself whom your cousin honours with his adoration. Is it the Honourable Emily?'

'I think Margaret is really the queen of his affections.'

'And what does she say to him—does she return the compliment? I should doubt whether a shallow nature like his could satisfy a character like hers. It is generous of me to praise her, for I know she cannot bear me. St. John has not got much beyond his Roman nose, and a certain fascination of manner to recommend him. There is a great deal of the cat in his nature.'

'Be quiet, you wicked creature,' cried Guendolen, now really displeased.

'So I must not say a word against its idol—very sorry—won't do it again'—and the artful widow crossed her hands with an air of mock penitence, which the girl was obliged to accept for fear of betraying any more of her own secret.

'I don't deny,' continued Sophy, 'that your cousin has some good points: he knows how to keep women in order, and that is a great thing. And though he has so many faults himself, he is rather clever at correcting the fair sex. If he married Margaret, she would not give him enough to do in that line.'

'Sophy,' said her friend, 'you can appreciate excellence so well, that I wonder you are not a better person yourself.'

'Thank you—it is the nature of the animal. I should be very sorry to be one of your goodies! I

intend to lead an awfully jolly life when I get
my little box at Richmond in order again, as I
hope to do in a month's time. You must be with
me a great deal then.'

'As much as I can, darling, rest assured.'

'But you haven't told me, and I want to know,
how Margaret behaves to St. John.'

'Why, she has become strangely reserved with
him. She will never walk out with him alone
now, as she used to do constantly. It makes
him very grumpy at times, the way she tries to
avoid him. He attempted to make her jealous
by devoting himself alternately to Emily and to
me. But she took it all in the sweetest way, as
if she was rather pleased. I think she is fond
of him, but in a very queer way. She used to
treat him as a brother, but that is at an end, for
what reason I know not.'

'I don't believe in any of that brother and
sister humbug,' remarked Mrs. Vivian.

'It would not suit you or me, Sophy, but I
think there are a few people who can go in for
that sort of thing.'

'How the devil must laugh at them,' chuckled the
widow, 'but I have a curiosity to know whether
your sister is inclined to favour Lord Fitzalan.'

'I don't believe she would marry a Protestant,
least of all a Unitarian.'

'Not if she really liked him?'

'No, she would conquer herself; Margaret has
great powers of self-sacrifice, and in womanly
pride I never met her equal.'

'She is a strange girl. She is as much an
enigma to me as Miss Fitzalan is.'

In the course of a few weeks, what with painters and upholsterers, Myrtle Cottage was transformed into an earthly paradise. The garden was laid out with taste, and the house was furnished with the utmost luxury. Mrs. Vivian and Guendolen had been enjoying an elegantly served luncheon together, in the cosiest of dining-rooms, when, looking out of window, the former beheld Lord Fitzalan riding by. On seeing her, he checked his horse, and she invited him to come in, promising that his steed should be cared for. He complied, and made himself most agreeable to both ladies.

'How is Emily?' inquired the younger one.

'I don't know,' he replied; 'she complained of a bad headache yesterday, which was Sunday, and stayed in her room most of the day. But her indisposition did not prevent her from taking a long walk in the cold, at some unearthly hour in the morning—so her maid informed me. I could get no satisfactory account, however, from my sister as to where she had been.'

'Can't you guess where she went?' inquired the widow. 'I thought there was but one heart and one soul between you. I would lay any wager you like that I find it out for you by this day week. What shall it be—a dozen pair of gloves?'

'Done!' said Lord Fitzalan. 'I must not refuse a lady's challenge.'

He regarded the matter simply as a joke on her part.

'And I vote that we three meet1 here for luncheon on Monday next,' said Mrs. Vivian.

The invitation was accepted, and during all that week she set her wits to work, in the most unscrupulous fashion, and at last ferreted out what she wanted to know. Guendolen remonstrated, but in vain, on the dishonour it would be to betray Miss Fitzalan's secret to her brother, and threatened to absent herself, though she longed to see the fun. But she was over-persuaded by her artful friend; and the trio thus strangely associated, met at Myrtle Cottage on the given day. Mrs. Vivian had provided a small but sumptuous repast that would have satisfied an epicure, which Lord Fitzalan was not. The champagne circulated freely, and, after the page had withdrawn, Mrs. Vivian laid before her noble guest a dainty glove of the palest lavender, and asked him if he recognised it.

'It is my sister's favourite colour,' he replied.

'Now guess where it was picked up,' said the lady.

'I have not the least idea,' said his lordship.

'In the Catholic Church at ——,' pursued Mrs. Vivian, 'on Sunday week last, at half-past seven in the morning; Miss Fitzalan having drawn it off for the purpose of approaching the altar to receive Holy Communion.'

A violent expression burst from the lips of Lord Fitzalan. At that moment he felt as if he hated Mrs. Vivian for the information which she had provided for him, procured, as it must have been, by unworthy means.

'Ladies, I must beg to be excused,' he said; 'this matter must be seen to without delay.' The strong man had become in a moment pale as death; he bowed his adieux, and left the room. But at the hall-door he turned, went back to the dining-room, and addressing his hostess with an exaggeration of politeness bordering on sarcasm, said: 'You will oblige me, madam, by giving me your number in gloves.'

'Six and a quarter,' said the widow, surprised that, under the weight of such a blow, he could remember a trifle.

But nothing was insignificant to Lord Fitzalan where his word was concerned.

'Sophy, I don't think he likes you the better for the service which you have done him,' remarked Guendolen, as soon as the door was closed.

'It was the spirit of mischief which possessed me,' said Mrs. Vivian; 'at all events, that sly girl will be punished. What business had she to give herself airs to me?' and there was an expression of wicked triumph in her eyes as she spoke, though she felt that she had burned her own fingers in perpetrating this act of revenge; for Lord Fitzalan had been inclined to like her, and now she had ruined herself in his good opinion.

As soon as he arrived at Stuart House, he went to his library, and despatched a message to his sister, which brought her to him at once. Her heart misgave her the moment she entered the room, but she seated herself calmly in an easy chair by the fire.

'Miss Fitzalan, what devil has been teaching you to deceive me?' he commenced.

'Pardon me,' she replied 'I have uttered no falsehood.'

'But you have suppressed truth infernally! You know what I mean. You have disobeyed me; and, above all, you have deceived me! Thank Heaven you are under age, and I have power to punish you!'

'I believe the law of the land would recognise my right to choose my own religion.'

'We shall soon see about that.'

'Oh, do not be angry with me!' said Emily, rising and advancing towards him with extended hands.

But, for the first time in his life, he put her away, and exclaimed:

'I am not going to stand any humbug! Tell me, in one word, will you renounce the Roman Catholic faith, or will you not?'

'Never!' she replied, in a voice which, though gentle, was as firm as his own.

'Then take the consequences, for I renounce you!'—he was almost beside himself with passion.

'I will go away, and live elsewhere, if that is what you wish,' said Emily.

'You shall be taken somewhere where you do not wish to go.'

He drew out his watch, made a calculation, rang the bell, and gave orders that Miss Fitzalan's maid should appear.

'Pack up immediately all your mistress's things,' he said to the girl; 'for she is going to Scotland by the night train.'

The young woman was fairly frightened, and asked: 'Am I to go, too, my lord?'

'No; your services will not be required.'

Emily could not forbear an appealing look at

her brother, but she had too much spirit to say a word before the servant. As soon as they were alone, he continued:

'I shall take you to your Aunt Maria, who, I fancy, will prove a strict châtelaine during the remaining months of your minority. When you are of age, I can no longer interfere with your liberty of action. Now go and take some refreshment, for the journey will be long and fatiguing.'

'How did you get to know this?' asked Emily.

'You came straight from Myrtle Cottage.'

'I decline to answer any questions. You must understand that you are in the deepest disgrace; and that you will be treated accordingly. Nothing short of a recantation will alter your sentence.'

'I didn't know that you were such a tyrant!' said Emily.

'You never put me to the test before, young lady. Even now I counsel you to think twice. You will find me inexorable.'

'Then I must make up my mind to banishment,' said Emily with decision, as she rose and left the room.

CHAPTER V.

THE brother and sister had a railway compartment all to themselves. When they had travelled for several hours without a word, Emily made an attempt to break the silence, but Lord Fitzalan stopped her by saying:

'You will oblige me by not addressing any conversation to me.'

The night sped on with dreary wings, and it was late in the afternoon of the next day before their journey was completed. Lord Fitzalan had sent a telegram to their aunt, that she might be prepared for their arrival at Glenross Castle. As soon as they got there, Lord Fitzalan gave orders that his sister should be shown to her room, while he alone entered the presence of Miss Glenross, who was an heiress in her own right. They were closeted together for an hour, at the end of which time the aristocratic spinster ascended to her niece's apartment. She was a clever lady, with a kindly heart where her prejudices were not concerned. She had been brought up in a strict Protestant school, and had been in the habit of regarding her nephew and niece as brands of perdition, for belonging to a different section from herself. Nevertheless, she had a certain affection for the former; and when he, relying on this attachment, came to her for assistance in a family difficulty, she was disposed to help him to the utmost. If she had been asked whether a Catholic or a Unitarian had the best chance of salvation, she would have replied 'The Catholic, I suppose.' She had a devout turn of mind, and was fond of the works both of Paschal and Fénelon. But with young people it was her opinion that discipline should be maintained, and this was a capital opportunity for taking her relative in hand, and converting her to her own way of thinking. She had given Lord Fitzalan a promise that no letter should reach Emily that had not been previously read by herself. She always kept the key of the post-bag.

Emily rose to meet her aunt, who only vouchsafed an icy touch of the hand, and remarked,

'I regret that the circumstance which has brought you to my roof should be so deplorable a one. But I trust that the time which you will pass with me may prove in every way profitable. I have assigned to you the same apartments which I occupied in my youth. The bedroom, as you see, is large and airy. The dressing-room, in which I shall expect you to spend your mornings, is provided with books of a solid and improving character. There is also a piano, so that you can keep up your music. In the afternoon, you will walk or drive with me; and in the evening we shall read together, so that no moment of the day need be unoccupied. You are probably tired after your journey. Would you like the refreshment of tea, or will you wait for supper, which will be served in an hour's time?'

'Please let me have a cup of tea, aunt, and then, with your permission, I will retire to rest.'

'Very well—I will send my maid to attend you. You have done right not to bring your own. I could not have tolerated a fine London lady playing her pranks in my quiet and orderly household. Good evening, niece.'

Miss Fitzalan, being wearied both in body and mind, slept the sleep of youth, and did not wake till, at seven o'clock, she received a brisk summons from her aunt's maid, who entered with a

lighted candle, and promised to return shortly to
help her to dress.

'I never get up by candle-light,' said the young
lady. 'Can I have a cup of tea?'

'Now, miss; while you are in bed?' asked the
astonished abigail.

'Yes, I am always accustomed to it,' said Miss
Fitzalan.

'There will be breakfast at eight to the click of
the clock, but I will speak to the housekeeper, and
see what I can do for you.'

In a few minutes Ruth returned, bearing a
cup of tea from the servants' breakfast-table.
At eight she reappeared with a tray containing
more solid refreshments, and said,

'Please, miss, it is my mistress's orders that
you have breakfast served in your dressing-room
for this once.'

Emily, who had scarcely begun her prayers,
was not sorry for this arrangement. Her sitting-
room, which communicated with her chamber,
had two windows looking different ways, and
commanding an extensive but dreary prospect.
It was a crisp January day; the fire had been
lighted, but the aspect of the room was somewhat
bare. The walls were well lined with books,
which was a consolation. There was a stiff
writing-table and high-backed chairs, but no spot
in the room where it was possible to be cosy.
To Emily, with her super-refined taste, and
extreme love for all that is elegant and pretty,
this was a bitter mortification. But she had
braced up her mind to learn the new lesson of
suffering, and she would not allow herself to be

discomposed. About noon, she sent a message, asking to see her brother. Ruth returned with the information that he was specially engaged. A little before one the maid reappeared with the news that dinner would be ready in a quarter of an hour. Would she please to come down when she heard the gong?

On entering the dining-room, she perceived that covers were only laid for two. As Miss Glenross was already at the head of the table, her heart misgave her, and after a formal greeting to her aunt, she anxiously inquired, 'Isn't Adrian coming?'

'Your brother took his departure half-an-hour ago,' said her hostess drily.

'And without bidding me good-bye!'

This was too much for Emily, and she burst into tears.

'Pray endeavour to command yourself,' said her aunt frigidly; 'there is nothing I dislike so much as a scene.'

Nevertheless there was a tear in the corner of the elder lady's eye. Emily did her best, and played with the slice of meat before her. The dinner passed in silence. When the cloth was removed, and the servant had withdrawn, Miss Glenross thus addressed her niece:

'It is better that I should tell you at the beginning that I permit no infringement of the rules of my household. I have been informed that you made an application for tea this morning at an unusual hour. I believe that modern fine ladies indulge in this beverage before they are out of bed in the morning. I consider it a sinful pampering of the body, especially in the case of young and healthy people. No such doings were ever heard of when I was a girl.'

'I shall certainly not transgress again, Aunt Maria,' said the niece. 'I fear that I have been somewhat spoiled; you see I have been mistress of my brother's house for two years, and I could do as I liked.'

'About the worst thing that could happen to any young woman. And I suppose that you had your full swing when you were travelling?'

'Yes, I did pretty much as I pleased.'

'Does Lady Sarah exercise any control over her household?'

'Lady Sarah is strict to herself, but indulgent to others. I never knew a person of her position who practises so much self-denial in the way of early rising and other things. But she does not exact the same standard from those around her. It is her great study to make people happy.'

'I suppose her young people are just as worldly as others?'

'They have the advantage of her example before them. Margaret, who has by nature an elevated mind, takes very much after her mother. I cannot say the same for Guendolen.'

'I am told that she is a very fast girl—more shame to her mother for allowing it.'

'I don't see the use of holding the reins too tight when people are grown up. It is not Lady Sarah's fault if her younger daughter has not profited by the advantages which she has had. She is a girl with a very strong will, and if she were too much thwarted now she would rebel openly.'

'As it is, I suppose she rebels secretly?'
'She has the highest esteem for her mother; but Lady Sarah would lose all her influence if she played the tyrant.'
'I should like to have the breaking-in of a girl like that,' remarked Miss Glenross, her eyes twinkling, 'provided she were a few years younger, so as to be within reach of the rod.'
'I think a severe system would have merely hardened her,' said Emily.
'I did not ask for your opinion, Miss Fitzalan. Now go and put on your things, if you please, and we will take a walk. It is too cold to drive.'

When Sunday came, and the carriage was announced, Emily, who knew of course where her aunt was going, steadily declined to accompany her. There was a good deal of altercation; both ladies got excited, but the younger one was firm, and carried her point, though it was very dull remaining at home. She occupied herself for some hours in solitary prayer and spiritual reading, for she had all her books with her, and took the precaution to keep them under lock and key. Her aunt always dined with the family under whose roof the Anglican service was conducted.

In the afternoon Miss Fitzalan strolled in the garden. She felt acutely the miseries of her position—torn away from all she loved, and from the means of grace. But she kept herself united to our Divine Lord, and offered up her crosses to Him, bracing herself up with the hope that the coming spring, if it did not end her trials, would at all events restore her liberty.

It generally happened that the Presbyterian

minister of the nearest village came to tea on the Lord's Day. He did his best to draw Miss Fitzalan into controversy, but she declined on the score that disputation was out of the question, when one party belonged to an infallible Church who could instruct, but could not debate. She alleged her own youth as an excuse for not answering any but the simplest questions. And this she did with an acuteness which surprised her interlocutor.

As time rolled on, Emily began to wonder that she had received no replies to the letters which she had written to the Bishop of Geneva. She need not have been surprised if she could have looked into her aunt's bureau, where the said letters peacefully reposed in a drawer. A few unimportant notes were occasionally handed to her by her aunt from different friends. After a while, Miss Fitzalan began to suspect the true state of the case, and instead of trusting her next epistle to the family bag, she slipped it into the post office. She had to wait several days before an opportunity occurred, for she was never permitted to walk or drive alone.

CHAPTER VI.

THE Mowbray family had suffered the greatest anxiety when they heard of Emily's sudden disappearance from the neighbourhood. Lord Fitzalan called at Lancester Court a few weeks after he left Scotland. He stated that he had placed his sister with a near relative, but beyond this fact he vouchsafed no information. He told Lady Sarah that as long as the young lady persisted in disobedience he must restrict her correspondence with her Catholic friends; although he deeply deplored the necessity he was under of acting in a way which he was 'aware must give pain to ladies whom he so highly esteemed.'

'Then it appears,' said Lady Sarah, 'that you claim for yourself personally the infallibility which you denounce as an extravagant assumption in the Catholic Church. You are inconsistent, my lord.'

'No I am not,' he said. 'If my sister were of mature age, say thirty, for instance, and were acting under no undue influence, I should say that she had a right to form her own views on religion, be they what they might. But, as it is, she is in *statu pupillari*—I need not apologize for speaking Latin to you. She is under my lawful authority, and I hold myself responsible for her. I do not choose that her mind and actions should be powerfully affected, for life, perhaps, by a change of religious belief, which I attribute mainly to the personal influence of a fascinating foreign prelate.'

'Then,' remarked Lady Sarah, 'if she perseveres in the faith which she has adopted, until she reaches what you choose to deem a sufficiently advanced age, you will withdraw your opposition?'

'I have no fear of that sort,' he replied. 'My sister is not fond of roughing it. A little wholesome discipline will soon bring her to her senses.'

His manner was so determined, as he rose and

took up his hat, that Lady Sarah could hardly bring herself to shake hands with him. But she remembered Emily's entreaties, that she would try to keep her influence over him, whatever might happen.

'Are you very angry with me?' he asked, turning back from the drawing-room door.

'Very angry,' she replied. 'I condemn your conduct on every principle of reason and justice.'

He had never seen such an expression of noble indignation upon any countenance. He had never admired her so much as he did at this moment.

'You do not know what it costs me to cross your wishes,' he said, once more touching the delicate hand which had always met his with friendship.

A tear started in the blue eyes which regarded him with a sort of maternal interest.

'You will be sorry for all this one day,' she said, ' and you will come back to me as a penitent.'

A smile that was not free from haughtiness curled his lip, but he only remarked :

'I do not think it likely. Farewell; do not let us part in anger; say something kind to a fellow!'

She could not help observing that either sorrow or anxiety had sprinkled a few grey hairs among his raven locks ; and she said to him in a softened tone: 'God be with you, Adrian!'

He kissed her hand as he might have done that of an empress, and hurried away.

About this time the Mowbray family were rejoiced by the return of the Colonel from India. The parting from her beloved husband had been an intense pain to Lady Sarah, but she had considered it her duty for the last few years to devote herself to her daughters, for whose health their native climate was essential. Colonel Mowbray was a noble specimen of an English gentleman. His appearance was aristocratic, and his manners were courtly. He was chivalrous and respectful to all women, from the highest to the lowest. His talents were such as would have won him distinction in any career that he might have chosen. Like all men of genius, he had certain peculiarities which were only saved from eccentricity by the high-bred grace of his manners and deportment. He was devoted to his Church, his sovereign and his country. In his varied travels he had found time to enrich his mind with the learning both of his own and of past ages. He possessed an irresistible attraction for the young. He was delighted to find himself again in the bosom of his family. His youngest daughter, Guendolen, was a cloud on his otherwise rich and beautiful life. The parents consulted together how to set her free from the snake-like influence of a certain widow who seemed to have a kind of mesmeric power over her. But the chain which bound these two young women together was so strong that it would require no ordinary power to break it.

St. John had been out of spirits for some time past, and he was usually remarkable for great buoyancy of mind. He was now living at his own place, which he had christened after himself, 'St. John Villa.' It was not more than a couple of miles from Lancaster Court. It was

furnished with the good taste of a gentleman
and the idealism of a poet. He had taken
great pains to prepare what he deemed a suitable
home for Margaret. But her continued coldness
and reserve at last convinced him that he had
no hope in that quarter. He then began to
dream of Emily's golden tresses. He left no
stone unturned to discover her address. He
managed to get hold of the county, and with the
assistance of a peerage book he contrived to
trace the name of Glenross. This was enough
for him to decide on a journey to the North.
When he got to the nearest post town, he took
up his abode at the hotel, and elicited from the
servants sufficient information to convince him
that a certain young lady who had been staying
at the Castle for about three months, was no
other than Miss Fitzalan. He ventured as far as
the village, and caught sight of the two ladies as
they drove past in the carriage. He calculated
that Sunday would be his best day to find Emily
alone, having ascertained that Miss Glenross
always drove to her own place of worship on the
first day of the week.

It was a warm April afternoon—an unusual
anticipation of summer. He did not dare to
approach the house too nearly, but he exercised
his powerful vision from afar. He had waited
about half an hour, watching every door and
window, when his patience was rewarded by the
gleam of a white *piqué* dress in the sunlight,
descending some steps into the flower-garden.
St. John advanced, and did not hesitate to
spring over the wall. He walked behind Emily,

crunching the gravel that she might have notice of somebody's approach. She turned and beheld him.

'Emily!' he exclaimed; 'dear Emily, do not be alarmed; I have come to save you!'

'Mr. Munro!' she cried in astonishment, 'have you fallen from the clouds?'

'No,' he said; 'but I am grieved to find how much you are changed. You have grown pale and thin. Now, do not attempt to deny that you are unhappy.'

'And have you come all this way for the sole purpose of helping me?'

'Is that surprising?' he asked, with a radiant smile, which transfigured his whole countenance.

'I am deeply indebted to you,' she replied; 'but I do not see how you can assist me.'

'I have a carriage here close by, and I will take you away with me. By to-morrow night I promise to convey you in all honour to Lady Sarah Mowbray. I know for certain that your brother is in Paris at the present moment. Once arrived at Lancaster Court, you can concert what measures you please with your friends.'

It was a great temptation certainly. Emily paused for a few moments before she replied:

'I thank you heartily, Mr. Munro. I should have no scruple in rebelling against the authority of a brother who is arbitrary in the use of his power; but I cannot bring myself to take a step which might compromise me in his opinion and in that of others.'

'Give me the right to protect you then!' cried St. John impetuously. 'Permit me the honour of escorting you as my betrothed wife.'

'This is too sudden,' said Emily, who was now red as a rose. 'Pardon me if I cannot accept your kindness.'

'Emily, this is folly. You must not make a martyr of yourself without necessity. I tell you plainly that I love you, and ask you to be my wife.'

'Are these fit words for me to listen to? A bird of the air told me that a dear friend of mine had a better right to have such a proposal made to her.'

The hot blood mounted to St. John's brow. He did not like to acknowledge that Margaret, with her high sense of honour, had by her studied coldness prevented the offer which he had longed to make. However, there was no escape, and he replied, 'I did not choose to press a suit which I saw was distasteful to my cousin.'

'Are you quite sure?' said Emily.

'Quite sure,' he replied. 'You may spare yourself all scruples of loyalty and delicacy on that point.'

'Your change of allegiance has been somewhat sudden,' she remarked; 'or was it merely a piece of Quixotism, to rescue a damsel in distress?'

She looked very lovely as she asked this question, an expression of pathos softening all her charms and enhancing them, unconsciously to herself.

St. John was greatly excited. He longed to take her in his arms and comfort her. But he stood awed before the innocence and dignity of her maidenhood.

'Why do you torture me with doubts?' he asked. 'Is it not enough that I adore you, that I would lay down my life for you? You would be as safe under my escort as under that of your own brother.'

'I do not doubt it,' she said; 'but at the same time I refuse to act in a way that would expose me to just criticism.'

'No one could presume to criticise the conduct of a lady who travelled under the care of her affianced husband.'

'And do you think,' she asked with a touch of hauteur, 'that my affection can be won in a moment, and that I can act in the precipitate way which you recommend?'

'My life shall be spent in proving that I am not unworthy of your confidence.'

The stateliness of her manner relaxed. There was something sweet, after months of desolation, in the offer of such devotion.

'Mr. Munro, I am really grateful to you for the kindness of your intentions,' she said, brushing away a tear which had risen.

The gentleness of her manner gave him boldness.

'Look here, Emily,' he said, 'I can arrange for our marriage before we leave this place. I cannot bear to leave you here alone.'

But she shook her head.

'It is not impossible for you to like me, is it?' he said, in his most attractive way.

'I do not know,' she replied. 'I could not make up my mind about anything so important, unless I had plenty of time.'

His hazel eye grew splendid with hope.

'But,' she continued, 'Mr. Munro ——'

'Call me St. John,' he interrupted.

'I cannot pledge myself as to the answer which I might give to your proposal under different circumstances, and after a longer acquaintance.'

St. John began to triumph in his own mind.

'The citadel will surrender at discretion,' he said to himself. 'I have a great inclination to try a bold stroke.'

He had been in the habit of frequently finding himself the only man among a party of ladies, and he had often domineered over his fair cousins. It was only of late that Margaret had thrown off the practice of yielding to him.

'Now, Emily,' he said in a decided tone, but with a manner perfectly respectful, such as might have been assumed by an elder brother; 'let us have no more nonsense, but just come along with me. When I have placed you under Lady Sarah's wing, I shall have accomplished a sacred duty, and you will have plenty of time to make up your mind about all the rest.'

He attempted to take her hand and lead her away, but she stood her ground with spirit.

'Mr. Munro,' she said, 'you will put me under the disagreeable necessity of summoning the butler. I shall not hesitate to do so if you behave in this way. And now, if you have anything more to say, you had better come into the house and say it, as I prefer that you should take your departure from the front door. I venture no conjectures as to the quarter from which you entered;' and there was a saucy look in her fine grey eyes, as she raised them to his.

'She is game to the back-bone,' he thought. He was not deficient in manliness, and liked her all the better for her courage. 'I would give a good deal,' he said to himself. 'to have that girl madly in love with me, and then to break her in.' Aloud, he only said, 'Lead the way, fair lady, and I will do your bidding.'

'I think our people will be returning from their place of worship, so I advise you to beat a speedy retreat,' said Miss Fitzalan, as she preceded him up the flight of steps which led into the library, whence she showed him the way to the hall-door. The ancient seneschal was snoring in an arm-chair.

'I think I may dispense with the ceremony of waking that individual,' said St. John in a subdued voice to Emily. 'Farewell for the present;' he bowed with a courtly grace, opened the front door, and was gone.

CHAPTER VII.

Mrs. Vivian and Guendolen were forming their speculations at Myrtle Cottage on the sudden departure of St. John.

'Did your cousin give any clue as to where he was going?' asked the former lady from the luxurious couch on which she was reposing.

'No,' said her companion; 'but I am sure that he is gone to see that horrid girl;' and as she spoke a dark expression came over her countenance.

'He is a good-for-nothing fellow, in my opinion,' said the widow.

'I forbid you to say a word against him—remember that, Sophy!'

'The Honourable Emily Fitzalan is the incarnation of cunning,' continued Mrs. Vivian. 'I should not wonder if there was an understanding between them, all this time.'

'I would give something to know that. By-the-by, did Fitzalan remember to send your gloves?'

'He did. The wretch is punctilious in trifles, and wounds me in serious matters whenever he has the chance. He has never called here since.'

The conversation was here interrupted by the entrance of the page with coffee. Mrs. Vivian prided herself on having the best of everything, and she certainly possessed the virtue of hospitality in a high degree. She had some good materials in her: she was generous and confiding when she really took to a person. But it is a deplorable fact that she had been deliberately unfaithful to the grace of a religious vocation which Almighty God had given her. This is a dreadful position for any human soul to be in. She had turned her back on the high favour which her Maker had proposed to her, and by so doing she had fallen into a state of sin through which, unless she repents in time, she will make shipwreck of her eternal salvation. At present, she is doing all she can to stifle the voice of conscience by inebriating herself with the pleasures of the world. She had taken a great fancy to Lord Fitzalan. She knew that he was poor for his rank in life, but she had no objection to a coronet.

While the two ladies were sipping the most delicious mocha, Guendolen looked across the little round table at her friend, and said :

'This charming scene, this lovely drawing-room, with your choice conservatory, must be a contrast to the convent!'

'A most agreeable one, I assure you. But to you, though to no one else in the world, I don't mind acknowledging that there is a thorn in the rose—that my heart often aches in the midst of all these pleasant things, for I know that I ought not to be here ; but I cannot make the sacrifice— I cannot give up this beautiful world—no, not for any amount—even of eternal bliss ! Between you and me there need be no humbug, which is a relief.'

'Because we know each other, and can make allowance for each other's little weaknesses. But I wish that you would put that nonsense of a vocation out of your head : you are no more obliged to be a nun than I am.'

'I wish that were true,' said the widow, as she brushed a tear from her eye.

Guendolen flew to her side, and kissed her tenderly.

'You are a sweet thing, Guen, and you know that I enjoy being petted,' said the elder lady. 'I am not fit to rough it. I could be good if I might have perpetual sunshine. As it is, I know that I am doing wrong, but I mean to get all I can out of Lucifer in this life—pretty dresses, and nice little dinners, and good operas——'

'And a handsome husband,' supplied Guendolen.

'I do not despair,' said the widow, with a meaning look. 'I think I know how to get round the men, which is more than you girls can do. If I cared for St. John as much as you do, I would have hooked him by this time. But then I am not bound by the proprieties; I am not the daughter of Lady Sarah Mowbray.'

'What do you mean to insinuate?' asked Guendolen.

'I insinuate nothing; but I have a scheme in my head. I have a great mind to run down to Scotland and see what they are up to. I believe if I could stop any serious mischief on the part of St. John, I should earn Fitzalan's gratitude.'

'But would not such a journey excite a great deal of attention?' asked Guendolen, who was deeply interested.

'My dear, I intend to travel *en garçon*, which will excite no attention whatever.'

'Oh, Sophy—you don't mean it——'

'Now don't be horrified prematurely, Miss Mowbray. I am not going to assume inexpressibles. But I shall take my long black convent cloak with me, a short skirt, and a pair of nailed boots. If you could only see me in that costume, in the dark, with my slouching Spanish hat, you would say that I look awfully like a young fellow.'

'I can quite imagine it,' said Guendolen.

'And I can handle a pistol better than most

men :' with these words, Mrs. Vivian jumped off
her sofa, vanished from the room, and reappeared
in the above-named habiliments, threw herself
into a martial attitude, and cried, 'Stand and
deliver!'

Guendolen laughed, and praised her cleverness.

'I suspect,' said she, 'that this is not the first
time that you have been guilty of a masquerade.'

'No, it is not. In the lifetime of the dear
departed, he and I went in for a lark now and
then.'

A few days after this conversation, Mrs. Vivian
set off on her journey. She had no great difficulty in tracing Mr. Munro's route, for, of course,
she had some vague idea of the locality of Glenross
Castle. When she reached the post town, having
no luggage except a travelling-bag and hat-box,
she went out to reconnoitre. People thought her
an eccentric lady of the middle class, a traveller
in search of the picturesque. She soon discovered
a farm-house, at about a mile's distance, at which
she could be lodged; and in the course of a day
or two she made herself mistress of St. John's
movements. She put most of her luxuriant hair
out of sight, and contrived so to change her com-
plexion that no one meeting her even by daylight
would have recognised her.

Having ascertained that Miss Glenross and her
suite always drove to a certain mansion, where
there was a religious meeting on Sunday, she
guessed that Mr. Munro would select that day
for his purposes, and she waited accordingly.
Chance favoured her more than she had hoped
for. It happened about the middle of the week

that Miss Glenross, having a bad cold, could not leave the house, and thought proper to send her niece in the carriage, attended by her own maid, to execute some commissions for her, having given directions that Ruth was not to lose sight of her charge for a moment.

Miss Fitzalan had a good deal to do at the draper's, and sent back the maid to pick up a brooch which she had dropped purposely in the millinery department upstairs. The post-office was close by. Emily inquired if there were any letters for the Castle. There was one for her aunt, which she kept in her hand, and another for herself, with a foreign post-mark, 'To be left till called for.' She had just time to put it in her pocket, when Ruth appeared. They both re-entered the carriage and drove off.

At that moment, strange to say, the postmistress discovered another letter addressed to 'The Honourable Emily Fitzalan, Glenross Castle.' She was lifting her voice to stop the carriage, when a tall figure appeared from the adjoining door, in a cottage-bonnet, robed in black, and thickly veiled, who said, in a well-trained voice, 'I am going to the Castle, and will see that the letter is safely delivered.'

The official thought that she might trust so respectable a person, and so refined a voice, and gave it up without hesitation.

Sophy proceeded on her way rejoicing, for she had recognised St. John's handwriting in a moment. She walked about half a mile in the direction of the Castle, and then turned off to the farm-house, where she soon ensconced herself

The Brides of Kensington. 57

in her chamber, and murmured to herself, 'This is delicious!' She speedily broke the seal, and read as follows:

'Crown Hotel.

'DEAREST EMILY,
    'I entreat you to reconsider the proposal which I made you ten days ago. I shall call upon you in due form next Sunday, ringing at the front door in the most orthodox way. If grey-beard refuses to admit me, I shall just put him aside. I will have a carriage in readiness.
'Yours devotedly,
'ST. J. M.'

'This is worth more than silver and gold to me,' thought Mrs. Vivian.

She sat down to the table, placed the inkstand before her, and indited an ingenious epistle to Lord Fitzalan, explaining how it had come to her knowledge that his beloved sister was in danger from certain plots and machinations. That the strange mystery of the case, together with the deep interest which she could not help feeling in one so engaging as Miss Fitzalan, had prompted her to do an extraordinary thing, viz., to make a journey to Scotland, solely with a view of watching over that young lady's welfare; and that Providence had favoured her with conclusive evidence of the perils which were besetting his sister. She added a promise that she would continue to exercise her gentle surveillance, at any inconvenience to herself, until such time as Lord Fitzalan could take steps for the more effectual protection of his treasure. She enclosed the letter which she had intercepted, declaring that it had been brought to her, and that she had opened it by mistake.

When Sunday came, she watched St. John to the door of the Castle, and saw him enter. He bribed the porter, who showed him into the library, and summoned Miss Fitzalan. She was greatly astonished, but thought it better to see him. The expression of surprise on her countenance induced her visitor to exclaim, 'Didn't you get my letter?'

'No,' said the young lady, somewhat alarmed; 'my aunt always opens the post-bag herself, and stops any letters to me that she does not approve of. I have just made that discovery.'

The epistle which she had lately got from Monseigneur Mermillod, and which had filled her with consolation, had also informed her that he had received no letter from her excepting the last.

'And do all your letters come in that horrid bag?' inquired St. John.

'All,' she replied, 'unless when the carriage goes to town, and the letters are called for, as we get them a few hours sooner. My aunt generally receives them in her own hand.'

'It is very strange,' said St. John, reflecting that if the document in question had fallen into the hands of Miss Glenross, it was improbable that she would have left her premises unguarded.

The same idea crossed Emily's mind, and she added: 'Last Thursday, my aunt being unwell, I called myself at the post-office, and certainly there was no letter from you.'

'And yet that is the very day when there should have been,' said Mr. Munro.

He then repeated his entreaties that she would avail herself of his escort, and resume her liberty. But Emily was firm, and insisted that he should make no further attempts to see her, as it would only embarrass her, and in no wise alter her resolution. After a great deal of arguing and pleading, he was obliged to leave her.

As he went out of the gate, he caught sight of a slouching hat behind a heap of wood. 'Holloa!' he cried, 'who's there?' But there was no reply. 'That's not a fellow from these parts,' thought St. John, who saw nothing but a long black cloak, a pair of men's boots below, and a Spanish sombrero above. The figure had just turned his back, and had evidently been on the watch. Mr. Munro approached, and laid his cane with no light touch across the shoulders of the intruder. 'Take that for eaves-dropping, my lad!' were his words.

The offender made off at a rapid pace.

Mrs. Vivian's letter to Lord Fitzalan reached him soon after his return from Paris. He was suffering from a low fever, and felt unequal to travelling, but he wrote as follows:

'DEAR MRS. VIVIAN,
        'You have secured my eternal gratitude for your good services. Unfortunately, I am too unwell to move, or I should lose no time in coming to the North, and administering a good horse-whipping to that scoundrel. As things are, I commission you to act for me. Oblige me by

calling on Miss Glenross; tell her all that has
passed, and that you are empowered by me to
undertake the charge of my sister, and to bring
her home with you.

'Your ever grateful
'FITZALAN.'

Sophy was indeed triumphant when she read
this letter. She congratulated herself on her
own cleverness. Meanwhile, St. John, seeing that
the case was hopeless for him, returned to his
own home. To the ladies at Lancaster Court he
gave no account of his journey or of its object;
but he was somehow startled to find that Mrs.
Vivian was absent from the neighbourhood.

'Where is she gone?' he inquired of Guendolen,
who thought proper to walk back with him as
far as their own lodge gate.

'How should I know?' said that young lady
demurely.

'I thought that you two were as thick as
thieves?' was St. John's irreverent remark.

'She told me that she was going to take a
little frisk, and I abstained from impertinent
questions.'

Do what she might, Guendolen could not help
colouring violently.

'You know all about it, I see,' said her cousin,
'so it is of no use telling me any lies.'

'St. John, I never tell lies! How dare you
say so!' and she stamped her pretty foot on the
gravel.

'Then you are a wonderfully deep young lady
for a truthful one—that is all I can say.'

The Brides of Kensington. 61

This interview, short as it was, sent him home more puzzled than ever. But his astonishment increased when, a few days after, he heard the news that Miss Fitzalan had returned to Stuart House, accompanied by Mrs. Vivian. Miss Glenross had taken a vehement dislike to the latter lady, who, of course, made her appearance at the Castle, properly attired in black silk, for she had sent for some luggage when she found that she was likely to be detained in Scotland beyond a few days. There was no disputing the written orders of Lord Fitzalan; so Emily was given up to the widow's escort, reluctantly on the part of her aunt, who, when she heard the whole story of St. John's invasion and Sophy's espionage, looked upon her niece as decidedly more sinned against than sinning.

Emily was so delighted to get back to her home that she tolerated the companionship of Mrs. Vivian, which would have been otherwise odious. She found her brother in a strange state of prostration. Men are helpless beings in sickness, and he was pleased to have his sister near him once more. She went up to his room, as if nothing painful had happened between them, kissed him affectionately, and commenced her duties as a nurse. She devoted herself to him with the most assiduous care. For some days he was in real danger. His cold philosophy could not enable him to face the possibility of death with calmness. He felt like a blind man groping for an invisible arm to support him.

He rallied, however, and one day he requested his sister to write and ask Lady Sarah to come and see him. Of course, Colonel Mowbray was consulted, and thoroughly approved of the scheme.

The room had been made to look particularly pretty and cheerful; the invalid's couch had been wheeled towards an open window, in the recess of which there was a table with a vase of exquisite flowers, and an easy-chair waiting for an occupant. Lord Fitzalan received his friend with the utmost warmth and gratitude.

'How good of you to come and see me after all my misconduct!' he said, with a ghastly attempt at a smile.

'I am so glad that you admit yourself to have been in the wrong. I am pleased with your generosity,' said his visitor.

'This dear girl,' he said, waving his hand towards Emily, 'has made me a noble return for all my unkindness and tyranny to her.'

'Don't speak of it, dearest,' said his sister tenderly; 'it has been a pleasure to me.'

'I believe it,' he said; 'and now you can take a nice walk in the garden, and try to get back your roses, which will give Lady Sarah an opportunity of reading me the lecture which I deserve.'

'You don't seem much afraid of it,' said Emily with an arch smile, as she vanished from the room.

There were many things which Lord Fitzalan could say to a non-relative as to the state of his mind on religious subjects, which he felt reluctant to broach with his sister. Lady Sarah had a very clear and powerful mind, in connection with the utmost tenderness of heart and gentleness of manner. He drew her out, to explain to him the supernaturalness of the Catholic Faith as brought to bear upon the events of daily life. She made him understand, as he had never done before, the grand doctrine of the Divinity of our Lord Jesus Christ.

'I could pardon you all the rest of your belief, Lady Sarah,' he said; 'but it strikes me that you are guilty of polytheism. You are not aware of it, it seems, but in reality you worship three Gods instead of one.'

'No, my dear friend, the unity of God is impressed upon us as one of the great fundamentals of our belief. I do not deny that it is difficult to conceive three Persons in one and the same God. I wish that I were a theologian, and able to explain to you the ineffable beauty and wondrous truth which underlies this great mystery. An all-perfect Being contemplates Himself from Eternity, and by so doing begets the Second Person of the Adorable Trinity; from the mutual love of the Father and Son effloresces the Holy Ghost; and yet there is but One Divine Nature, but One God!'

'Do I understand you to say that the Holy Ghost is the effect of the mutual love of the Father and the Son?'

'Not so as to imply posteriority. But I should like you to talk to a priest. I have got a relation of mine, Father Adelbert, staying just now at our house. I shall bring him to see you if you will let me.'

'What you have told me is very wonderful and highly suggestive. I should like to have a few days to think it all over.'

Lady Sarah was of opinion that there had been
enough serious conversation for one day. So she
subsided into lively amusing chat about their
home affairs. In other words, she regaled him
with a spicy dish of clever innocent gossip, which
thoroughly refreshed his mind. She often went
to see him after this, and introduced Father
Adelbert to him, who, in process of time, completed the good work, and received Lord Fitzalan
into the Church. His was not a mind to be turned
by the painful process of minute investigation.
He was attracted by the majesty of a system
which penetrated his soul with a direct over-
whelming evidence of its own Divinity, as soon
as he had learned to know and to adore his
Creator.

The joy of his sister knew no bounds, and the
entire family of the Mowbrays joined in hearty
congratulation. He became an excellent Catholic.
The strength of character which had made him
a bitter opponent, now made him a zealous ad-
vocate of the truth. His talents, his influence,
all that he had, were offered up as a loving holo-
caust to the God Whom he had found—to the
Redeemer Who had so powerfully attracted him.
Months rolled away; summer was past, and
autumn, rich and glorious, was taking its place.
He took an early opportunity, after his recovery,
of driving over to Myrtle Cottage. He had
wished his sister to accompany him in this visit,
but Emily steadily refused to countenance a lady
who had been guilty of such dishonourable conduct as Mrs. Vivian's had been. She had ex-
plained everything to her brother, who saw plainly

that St. John's behaviour was not so unpardonable as he had supposed it to be. When the two gentlemen met, there was no allusion made to the past on either side.

Mrs. Vivian hated Mr. Munro more than ever. It seemed as if she still felt in her soul the sting of St. John's cane. It was an inexpiable offence, all the more so because it was a case in which no satisfaction could be demanded. He knew right well how matters stood, but his manhood prevented him from acknowledging to anyone that he had, though unwittingly, chastised a lady. He took every opportunity of paying court to Emily, who for a long time received his attentions with the utmost coldness.

When Lord Fitzalan paid the visit which he considered due on his part to Mrs. Vivian, he found her in the drawing-room alone and pensive. He made his acknowledgments once for all, but with less fervour than she had expected, and began to talk on indifferent subjects. This did not suit the young widow's purpose; she was resolved to be confidential; so she presently turned the conversation on his sister, and affected to regret her own misfortune in failing to gain the regard of 'so charming a girl.'

'I am very sorry,' he said politely, 'but I suppose that my sister must be left to choose her own friends. Ladies, you know, will not be dictated to in such matters.'

'But if you have an opportunity of using your influence,' she remarked in her most caressing way, 'Miss Fitzalan looks up to you so much, and deservedly—you would suggest to her, would you not, dear Lord Fitzalan, in the most gentle and natural way, what a sincere and devoted friend she would have in me?'

Sophy raised her fine eyes to his, and they were swimming with tears. She took care, however, not to let them fall, for they would have spoiled the effect of her pearl powder. She looked so artless, so handsome, and so alluring—what could a man do but promise anything she asked? She thanked him with effusion, and the interview was becoming highly interesting to both of them, when there came a sound from the garden as of visitors arriving. The door opened, and the Miss Mowbrays were announced. They wore black silk dresses beautifully made, and white straw hats with ostrich plumes.

'I hope you will kindly excuse me, Mrs. Vivian, if I only stay a few minutes,' said Margaret; 'but mamma has granted me the pony carriage this afternoon to go and see a friend at Kensington. Guendolen wished me to drop her here on the way, and with your permission I will call for her as I return in the evening.'

'No; I cannot accede to that,' said Sophy. 'You must leave her here for the night. I cannot consent to part with her sooner.'

'Very well,' said Guendolen to her sister, 'you need not trouble yourself to pick me up, dear.'

'Mamma would prefer——' began Margaret.

'I quite agree with a gentleman who said that "mamma is a word that ought to be banished from the lips of young ladies,"' remarked Guendolen saucily. 'Have I shocked you, Lord Fitzalan?'

'Rather,' he replied. 'You are aware of my Conservative principles, and that I have a respect for old institutions.'

'Old institutions may be good, but young ones are better, or, at least, prettier,' said Mrs. Vivian, with an expressive glance from her favourite to Lord Fitzalan, who, however, turned to Miss Mowbray, and said:

'Will you permit me to accompany you part of the way?'

'Certainly,' said Margaret, with heightened colour; 'and I am afraid that I have no time to lose.'

She made her adieux to Mrs. Vivian with the utmost courtesy, indeed with rather more ceremony than she would have shown to a person whom she liked. Mrs. Vivian looked after them as the gentleman put the lady into the carriage, and requesting the coachman to take the back seat, assumed the reins and drove off. It was provoking to see her lawful prey, as she deemed him, departing from the sphere of her fascinations: for though fully conscious of her own advantages, she had the sense to feel that she was not a match for Miss Mowbray, either in beauty or high breeding. She bit her lips to conceal her mortification, which her companion perceived in a moment.

'He takes the reins,' observed Guendolen, 'with the air of a master, as if he would like to drive through life at my sister's side.'

'Does she care for him?' anxiously inquired the widow.

'Do you think that she would condescend to

show, or even to indulge a preference, until his lordship had declared himself? You might as well expect the statue of Juno Regina to forget her goddess-ship!'

'I don't like that marble style of woman, with more head than heart.'

'There you are mistaken: if Margaret were really in love, she would love more intensely than you or I would; her affection would be more concentrated from never having been wasted in flirtations. But I am in no mood for metaphysical speculations—sit down and give us a song.'

'I will give you a tune, if you like,' said Mrs. Vivian, who was not inclined for further conversation.

They took a drive to see Madame Elize's new dresses before dinner. In the meantime Adrian and Margaret had enjoyed a delightful conversation. He had done his best to entertain his fair companion, and had drawn her out into a delicious interchange of thoughts and ideas; for Miss Mowbray's mind was highly original and well stored. Few men could be more fascinating than Lord Fitzalan, when he chose to be so. He possessed the subtle charm of mental power in connection with great personal advantages. On this occasion he wished to make sure of his ground before committing himself to a proposal. As he handed her out of the carriage, he said in a marked way:

'May I be permitted to call on you to-morrow afternoon?'

'I think you will find us at home,' said

Margaret, with a bright blush and a frank genial smile.

'Good-bye till then,' he said, resigning the delicately gloved hand which he had held in his own while he spoke.

Their eyes met: there was something of the proud triumph of a possessor in the expression of his countenance, before which Margaret's glance sank abashed, but not displeased. These two were beginning to understand each other so well that they could dispense with superfluous words.

CHAPTER VIII.

ALL that night Mrs. Vivian tossed about on her couch concocting schemes. She would not give up the game, desperate as it seemed, she was playing for too high a stake. She resolved that she would show none of the jealousy by which her heart was torn. She would aim at being the confidential friend of Lord Fitzalan. Already she felt that she had a certain hold on him. It is sometimes agreeable to a man, as she knew right well, to have a lady friend to whom he can have the pleasure of talking of his beloved one. At breakfast-time she encouraged Guendolen to converse about St. John.

'He is just now out of spirits,' said the girl; 'he seems to be madly cracked about Emily; and she is a most wicked coquette. At times she is so kind to him, that it is enough to deceive a saint, and then she treats him with coldness. I try to convince him that it is labour lost, and that she does not care for him. But I never saw a man so infatuated.'

Now this statement was not altogether true. St. John was very deep. He saw that Emily's was a nature difficult to win, and that he lost ground by open love-making. So he studied to excite an interest in her mind; and she was so fond of pleasing, and so averse to giving pain, that she did not always discourage him. Besides, he knew better than Guendolen did, how to thread the mazes of that wonderful labyrinth— a woman's soul!

Mrs. Vivian pondered for a few minutes before she replied to the speech which we have recorded above.

'I think I can help you,' she said at last; 'I have some influence over Adrian, and I will work on his sense of honour, and convince him how wrong it is on the part of his sister to encourage hopes which she has no intention of realizing; and I know the alliance would be hateful to Fitzalan.'

Sophy did not take Guendolen home till late in the afternoon; and just as they drove up to the lodge-gate, they beheld Lord Fitzalan and Margaret strolling in the shrubbery. They both came forward; Guendolen sprang from the phaeton, and saluted her sister. Lord Fitzalan greeted Mrs. Vivian with his usual high-bred unembarrassed manner.

'Am I to congratulate you?' asked the widow in her sweetest voice, with a deceitful smile.

'You may indeed,' he said, 'I have won the best girl in Christendom!' and his eye rested on Margaret with a lover's joy and pride.

'I wish you happiness,' said Mrs. Vivian; 'I thought Miss Mowbray had other views. I understood that there was some talk of a vocation about a year ago.'

Lord Fitzalan looked slightly annoyed, but replied: 'I am not robbing the sanctuary, Mrs. Vivian. All that was settled long ago. Margaret took the best advice upon the subject, and it was decided that she was to remain in the world.'

'Adieu!' said Sophy. 'I must be returning home to receive visitors. Will you kindly tell Guendolen that I am going.'

He did her bidding, and then asked Margaret to come and do the polite to her sister's friend.

'I had rather not,' she said. 'Mrs. Vivian is a person whom I should positively hate, if it were not a sin to do so. I have already spoken to her, and wished her good morning.'

He looked at her gravely.

'Margaret,' he said, 'you must conquer yourself in this matter. Mrs. Vivian is a friend of mine.'

'Oh, no!' she said impetuously. 'I do not believe it.' Her eye flashed and her colour rose. 'The thing is impossible,' she added; 'there can be nothing in common between her nature and yours.'

'Nevertheless, I ask you to show me this favour,' and his voice had an accent of command in it.

Margaret looked up—there was a rebellious tear in her dark hazel eye—but he did not relent.

'Come with me,' he said, 'and receive Mrs. Vivian's congratulations in your most graceful way.'

'Oh, Adrian!' she said; but he took her hand with an air of authority, placed it under his arm, and led her to the gate, where the proceeding had been closely watched by Sophy and Guendolen.

'His lordship is beginning to play the tyrant already, and it is early days,' whispered the former, who could not hear a word of the colloquy. 'I doubt whether her high spirit will stand it—it ought to be the lady's rule now.'

'What a good thing it is that you are not under him,' said Guendolen mischievously.

But the other replied: 'I would make a pretence of submission during the engagement, and pay him off roundly as soon as I became his wife. Hush! they are coming.'

Margaret had the air of a princess as they approached the carriage. There was nothing to criticise in the perfect grace with which she accepted Mrs. Vivian's polite speeches. She saw through their hollowness; but she proffered her thanks without betraying that knowledge. She had her reward in a gratified smile from her betrothed.

'I shall expect you all to come and lunch with me to-morrow,' said Sophy, with her most captivating manner. 'Lord Fitzalan, I know that I may reckon on you; and will you oblige me by prevailing on your sister to accompany you without a formal invitation ?'

'Thanks, Mrs. Vivian; I will do my best,' he said significantly.

'Shall we say two o'clock then?' and she bowed gracefully to Margaret and Guendolen. The proper answer was made, and the widow took her departure.

Lord Fitzalan had a battle to fight with Emily that evening as they sat together after dinner. The fact of her brother's being engaged to her dearest friend was a source of real delight to her; but when she was told of the invitation, which he had accepted for the morrow, she flatly refused to make one of the party.

'On such an occasion, Emily,' he remonstrated, 'it will be thought most unkind if you absent yourself. What will Margaret say?'

'Margaret will understand my motives. My feeling against Mrs. Vivian is so strong, that nothing on earth shall induce me to enter her house as a guest. I am sorry that she has inveigled you into going. I suppose Margaret could not help herself? she is hardly a free agent now, which makes me all the more vexed that you have fallen into the trap.'

'My dear Emily, that is not a fair expression to use. A lady invites us to luncheon, for the purpose of doing honour to my betrothed, and you insist upon it that she has some sinister view.'

'May God forgive me if I am uncharitable,' said Emily; 'I do believe that she has some evil design.'

'What, with regard to an engaged man? You may as well speak out, and tell me your suspicions.'

'Adrian, I believe that woman has as many wiles as Lucifer. She has no friendly feelings in inviting me, for I know that she hates me; but she could not ask you very well, without including me. I do not venture to say what is her precise game at the present moment; but I am certain that she is madly jealous of Margaret. I have seen the expression of her face, on various occasions, when she was off her guard, and I warn you to beware. A woman's intuition is often better than a man's wisdom. If I could prevent Margaret from visiting her, I would.'

'Stop there, Emily. You are of age—you are mistress of your own actions. I do not attempt to interfere with you beyond giving my advice. But I forbid you to exercise any influence over Margaret in this matter. Of course she will now consult my wishes in all respects.'

'Why, that is reversing the order of things. It is the lady who rules during the time of engagement.'

'Is it, indeed? Then I shall make that time as short as possible.'

'You have just lost a subject in me,' said Emily, in a playful way; 'and you want some one else to tyrannize over, I do believe!'

'Ask Margaret if that is her opinion? It will be only charitable to warn her.'

'I shall do no such thing. Margaret is one of those high natures born to command, but yet

one who knows when she has found her master.
Where she loves deeply, she will instinctively
obey; but she will wear her chain with such
dignity and grace that no one will guess its
existence.'

'Well done, Emily! You know how to appreciate your friends. So you think I am a bit of a tyrant, after all!'

Emily came behind his chair, stooped over him with a look of admiring fondness, and imprinted a silent kiss on his open brow.

She wrote a politely worded excuse to Mrs. Vivian, which did not surprise that lady.

It was a very agreeable luncheon-party. Margaret felt so happy in the presence of her betrothed that it required no effort to be cordial to their hostess. The latter contrived to be alone with Lord Fitzalan, while the young ladies were putting on their hats, before returning home.

'When am I to congratulate Miss Fitzalan?' she began.

'About what?' inquired his lordship.

'Her engagement to Mr. Munro.'

'There is no such thing on the tapis—nor likely to be,' said her guest with decision.

'I fancy that St. John is of a different opinion. He boasts of having received encouragement of late. But, of course, I thought that you knew all about it, or I should not have made such an indiscreet remark. But then, you know,' she added, with a coaxing smile, 'young ladies cannot be expected to tell everything even to the best of brothers.'

'There was nothing to tell in this instance.'

'Then I can only suppose that Mr. Munro's self-conceit has magnified your sister's natural kindness and charm of manner into direct encouragement of his suit. If I were you, I should put her on her guard, for I know that he flirts desperately with his cousin Guendolen when he has the chance.'

'I think there must be some mistake—I am reluctant to believe this—but I will not fail to speak to my sister,' said Lord Fitzalan, feeling greatly annoyed.

He took the first opportunity of doing this, and told Emily, in his usual straightforward way, that she might lay herself open to the imputation of coquetry, unless she took care to repel the attentions of a certain gentleman in the neighbourhood.

'Mrs. Vivian has put you up to this, Adrian!' was the young lady's exclamation. 'It is one of her wicked tricks!'

'You do her great wrong,' said Lord Fitzalan; 'her counsel was given as a friend both to you and me. She had heard that you were already engaged to Mr. Munro.'

'I don't believe a word of it! She invented the story to suit some purpose of her own.'

'Of course I contradicted it in the most decided way; but you must be careful, dear, not to act in a manner that may give colour to such rumours.'

What feeling was it that made Emily rise from the dessert-table, where she generally lingered to chat with her brother when they were alone together? As he rose to open the door for her he observed that her colour was heightened, but he attributed this to the lecture which he had just administered.

'That woman wants to get me out of St. John's mind,' thought Emily, as she sat down in the drawing-room and took up a book mechanically,

CHAPTER IX.

MISS FITZALAN was still deep in thought when the footman entered, carrying a bouquet of the choicest hot-house flowers, with Mr. Munro's compliments to herself. Her brother came into the room in time to hear her say distinctly: 'Give my thanks and compliments to Mr. Munro; tell the servant to be sure and remember.'

Presently Adrian approached his sister, and looked at her with a steady inquiring expression. She met his gaze with a smile and a blush.

'Is it possible,' he asked, 'that a change has come over the spirit of the dream?'

'It is possible,' she replied.

'You have not been quite candid with me, my own sister, have you now?' he said with an accent of tender reproach, as he took his seat on the sofa by her side.

'You must forgive me,' she said, taking his hand and fondling it, as if she were caressing a dove.

'Well,' he said, 'I don't want to be hard upon a young lady! But St. John Munro is not the man whom I should have chosen for you.'

'Why not?' she asked.

'"Unstable as water, he will not excel!"'

'You cannot deny that he is clever.'

'Yes; but it is a shallow sort of cleverness—there is no depth in him. He has good points, and good impulses. There are times when he seems to be getting near the sun, and then he disappoints you by veering off into space.'

'I am sorry that you and I disagree on this subject,' said Emily with so much feeling that Adrian exclaimed:

'My darling girl, may you be happy; it is the only wish of my heart that he may turn out worthy of you!'

But the subject still seemed painful to him, and he left the room.

Miss Fitzalan had expected more decided opposition on his part, and was thankful to find that such was not the case. The change which had been wrought in her own mind during the last six months had been so gradual that she had been hardly conscious of it herself. She was very clever; she had a clear judgment; she knew that there was truth in every word which her brother had uttered, and that his censure was not too severe. But she had yielded to an overpowering fascination: she was under a spell. Happy would it have been for her at this crisis if she could have opened her whole mind to the Bishop of Geneva, and submitted her fate to his decision, or rather to the will of God, as it might be manifested through him.

The following afternoon St. John called and found Miss Fitzalan at home. He proposed in due form and was accepted. The next morning brought the important news in a letter from Emily to Margaret. The latter rejoiced with trembling, and lost no time in going over to see her friend. As Miss Mowbray entered the pony-carriage, which was to take her to spend the day at Stuart House, Guendolen made her appearance, looking deadly pale, and requested her sister to make a little detour, so as to put her down at Myrtle Cottage. Margaret guessed the origin of the poor girl's trouble, but she asked no questions, and showed her sympathy by the tenderness of her manner.

The 'Wedding March' was played superbly, on the fine midsummer morning when Lord Fitzalan and Margaret were united in holy matrimony at the High Altar of the Pro-Cathedral, Kensington, by His Eminence the Cardinal Archbishop of Westminster. The stately church was a perfect paradise of flowers. The newly married couple set off for the Continent with the intention of returning shortly to a happy home and a life of active duties. They came back in time to assist at another ceremony, in which Lord Fitzalan gave away his fair sister to St. John Munro. This wedding was less grand in outward appearance than the one which had preceded it, for such was Emily's special wish; but there were many loving hearts who prayed for her. Everything was arranged with perfect taste and solemnity by the Reverend Administrator who officiated

Perhaps at a future time our readers may hear something more of the persons who have figured in this history—and how it fared in after-years with the Brides of Kensington!

THE END.

R. WASHBOURNE, PRINTER, PATERNOSTER ROW, LONDON.

" A glance at Mr. Washbourne's lists will always acquaint us where we may find light, diverting Catholic literature."—*Catholic Book News*, Jan., 1881.

WASHBOURNE'S CATALOGUE

OF LIBRARY AND PRIZE BOOKS,

AND LIST OF WORKS IMPORTED

FROM AMERICA. See page 20.

COMPLETE CATALOGUE SENT POST FREE.

18 *PATERNOSTER* ROW, LONDON.

Post Office Orders to be made payable to
Robert Washbourne, at the General Post Office.

Father Placid; or, the Custodian of the Blessed Sacrament. By L. Oliver. 1s.

Rose Fortescue; or, the Devout Client of Our Lady of Dolours. By L. Oliver. 1s.

The Most Beautiful among the Children of Men— Meditations upon the Life of Our Lord. By Mrs. Abel Ram. With a Preface by the Cardinal Archbishop of Westminster. 3s.

For Better, *not* For Worse. A Tale of our own Times. By Rev. Langton George Vere. 3s.

A Friendly Voice; or, the Daily Monitor. By the author of "Golden Sands." 6d.

Second Series of True Wayside Tales. By Lady Herbert. 3s., or separately :—

Moothoosawmy, or Natural Uprightness Supernaturally Rewarded; Saveriammal, or the Story of a Snake-bite and its Cure; Father Koblyowicz, or the Martyr to Sacramental Silence. 1s.

Emily; Nancy; the Efficacy of Prayer; and the White Necktie, a Story of First Communion. 1s.

The Two Cousins; The Result of a Mother's Prayers; and The Two School-boys. 1s.

Our Esther. By M. F. S., author of "Jack's Boy." 2s. 6d.

The Gamekeeper's Little Son, and other Tales. By the author of " Bobbie and Birdie." 2s. 6d.

True Wayside Tales. By Lady Herbert. 3s.; or may be had separately, in 5 volumes, cheap edition, in pretty binding, price 6d. each volume.
1. The Brigand Chief, and other Tales. 2. Now is the Accepted Time, and other Tales. 3. What a Child can do, and other Tales. 4. Sowing Wild Oats, and other Tales. 5. The Two Hosts, and other Tales.

"These tales are short, in good legible type, and evidently true."—*Tablet.*

Chats about the Commandments. By M. F. Plues, author of "Chats about the Rosary." 3s.

"This book is written in a manner that would attract children, and we should think that it will be found a help by parents and teachers. . . . What you have written is very practical and true."—*Cardinal Manning.*

Jack's Boy. By M. F. S., author of "Tom's Crucifix, and other Tales," "Fluffy," etc. 3s.

"The author of 'Tom's Crucifix' is a favourite with many readers, old and young. There is a tender depth of feeling which runs through every page, and a simple earnestness and manifest truthfulness in the manner and style of the narration which renders her stories peculiarly attractive."—*Weekly Register.* "The more we have of such tales to move kind hearts, the better will it be for the children of the poor in our overgrown towns."—*The Month.*

Bertram Eldon and how he found a home. By M. A. Pennell, author of "Nellie Gordon." Cloth, 1s.

"Authors who will and can write little books like 'Bertram Eldon,' may hope to do much good thereby, for they are directly helping to inspire children with a love of the neglected poor, which will through after-life bear fruit in works of mercy."—*The Month.* "We can all learn a lesson from such a career as 'Bertie Eldon's.'"—*Catholic Times.*

Walter Ferrers' School Days; or, Bellevue and its Owners. By C. Pilley. 1s. 6d.

"A family suffers a sudden reverse of fortune by the death of the father and the dishonesty of his agent. The Christian matron shows herself equal to the occasion, and her children find strength in her example, derive benefit from adversity, and struggle forward into happier times."—*The Month.* "A tale for the young. Its incidents are so arranged as to inculcate the practice of honesty and virtue, and a trust in the goodness of Providence. The juvenile mind will delight in it."—*Catholic Times.*

The Golden Thought of Queen Beryl, and other Stories. By Marie Cameron. 1s. 6d., or may be had separately, cheap edition, in pretty binding, price 6d. each volume.
1. The Golden Thought, and The Brother's Grave.
2. The Rod that Bore Blossoms, and Patience and Impatience.

"Pleasantly written tales."—*Court Circular.*

Bobbie and Birdie; or, Our Lady's Picture. By Frances I. M. Kershaw. Fcap. 8vo., 2s. 6d.

Out in the Cold World. By M. F. S. (Mrs. Seamer), author of "Tom's Crucifix." 3s.

The Siege and Conquest of Granada. Allah Akbar—God is Great. From the Spanish. By Mariana Monteiro. 3s.

"A highly interesting story. The book is handsomely got up, and the illustrations, which are from the pencil of a sister of Miss Monteiro, add much to the beauty of the volume."—*Public Opinion.*

Gathered Gems from Spanish Authors. By Mariana Monteiro. 3s.

CONTENTS :—The Rosary Bell—The Blind Organist of Seville—The Last Baron of Fortcastells—The Miserere of the Mountains—Three Reminiscences—A Legend of Italy—The Gnomes of Monccay—The Passion Flower—Recollections of an Artistic Excursion—The Laurel Wreath—The Witches of Trasmoz.

"Genuine treasures of romance."—*Weekly Register.* "Particularly rich in pleasant stories of the purest morality."—*Irish Monthly.* "Of considerable beauty. . . . The high moral tone of it renders it far in advance of the majority of tales at the present day."—*Public Opinion.* "Much grace and freshness."—*University Magazine.*

The Last Days of the Emperor Charles V., the Monk of the Monastery of Yuste. An Historical Legend of the 16th century. From the Spanish, by Mariana Monteiro. 2s.

"An exceedingly interesting historical legend. It will amply repay perusal."—*Court Circular.* "A peculiar interest attaches to the tale."—*Weekly Register.* "It is well calculated to instruct and entertain the minds of young persons, since it is a tale of piety and also historical."—*Tablet.* "A very realistic picture of the character of Charles in monastic repose. We have read every page of the volume with much pleasure."—*Catholic Times.* "The whole narrative just the sort that might be put in the hands of a boy or girl under sixteen with advantage."—*Public Opinion.* "Well worthy of notice."—*The Month.*

The Battle of Connemara. By Kathleen O'Meara, author of "A Daughter of St. Dominick." 2s. 6d.

"Everything else is but a sketch, compared with the Irish scenes, which are written *con amore*, and though not very highly coloured, are faithful to life."—*Dublin Review.* "A charming story, charmingly told."—*Irish Monthly.* "A book which has interested us; in which others, we doubt not, will take much interest."—*Tablet.* "The sketch of the Holy Mass in the miserable thatched building is one of the most effective bits of description we have seen; and this portrayal of peasant life, privation, and faith is too accurate to be questioned."—*Catholic Times.* "This interesting tale."—*The Month.*

Industry and Laziness. By Franz Hoffman. From the German, by James King. 2s. 6d.

"This is a capital story for boys. We can assure youthful readers that they will find much to attract them in this adventurous story."—*Weekly Register.* "The moral is excellent, the interest of the story well sustained."—*Tablet.* "A good, moral story."—*Court Circular.* "Any book that tries to save boys and young men from copying the example of John Collins deserves to be encouraged, especially when it is so very readably written and printed as the present tale."—*Irish Monthly.*

The Fairy Ching; or the Chinese Fairies' Visit to England. By Henrica Frederic. Handsomely bound in cloth, 1s.

My Golden Days. By M. F. S. 12mo., 2s. 6d., or in 3 vols., 1s. each.
 The One Ghost of my Life, Willie's Escape, &c.
 The Captain's Monkey, &c.
 Great Uncle Hugh, Long Dresses, &c.

"They are playfully descriptive of the little ways and experience of young people, and are well suited for reading aloud in a family circle of juveniles."—*The Month.* "A series of short tales for children, by the delightful author of 'Fluffy' and a score of other charming books for the young."—*Weekly Register.* "Capital tales for children, nicely told, printed in large type on good paper and neatly bound."—*The Bookseller.* "Feelings run through them like a stream through flowers, and pretty morals peep out as the reader travels along."—*Catholic Times.* "This is the latest of the long catalogue of bright and edifying books of short stories for which our young people have to thank M. F. S."—*Irish Monthly.*

The Two Friends; or, Marie's Self-denial. By Madame d'Arras (*Née* Lechmere). 1s.

"A little French tale, in the crisis of which the good Empress Eugénie plays a conspicuous part."—*Weekly Register.*

Andersen's Sketches of Life in Iceland. Translated by Myfanwy Fenton. 1s. 6d.

"In the one case they are simply pretty tales; in the other curious illustrations of the survival to our own time of thought and manners familiar to every reader of the Sagas."—*Graphic.* "Ever welcome additions to the literary flora of a primitive and little-known country, such as Iceland must still be deemed. The Princess of Wales has been pleased to accept this unpretentious little story-book, written in the high latitudes where legends flourish abundantly."—*Public Opinion.* "Told with simple eloquence. A happy mean of refreshing simplicity which every reader must enjoy."—*Catholic Times.* "The style is fresh and simple, and the little volume is altogether very attractive."—*Weekly Register.*

George Lawson, or the Dark Shadow. A Tale. 2s. 6d.

Story of a Paper Knife. By Henrica Frederic. 1s.

Rest, on the Cross. By E. L. Hervey. Author of "The Feasts of Camelot," &c. 3s. 6d.

"This is a heart-thrilling story of many trials and much anguish endured by the heroine. Rest comes to her, where alone it can come to all. The little tale is powerfully and vividly told."—*Weekly Register.* "Mrs. Hervey has shown a rare talent in the relation of moral tales calculated to fascinate and impress younger readers."—*Somerset County Gazette.* "An interesting and well-written religious story for young people."—*The Bookseller.* "An emotional and gushing little novelette."—*Church Times.* "It is impossible for us to know how far the events and situations are real, and how far imaginary; but if real, they are well related, and if imaginary, they are well conceived."—*Tablet.* "It is written in the gentlest spirit of charity."—*Athenæum.*

The Feasts of Camelot, with the Tales that were told there. By Eleanora Louisa Hervey. 3s.

"This is really a very charming collection of tales, told as is evident from the title, by the Knights of the Round Table, at the Court of King Arthur. It is good for children and for grown up people too, to read these stories of knightly courtesy and adventure and of pure and healthy romance, and they have never been written in a more attractive style than by Mrs. Hervey in this little volume."—*Tablet.* "This is a very charming story book."—*Weekly Register.* "Mrs. Hervey brings the great legendary hero within the reach of children, but the stories are quite sufficiently well told to deserve the perusal of more critical readers."—*The Month.* "These tales are well constructed, and not one of them is destitute of interest."—*Catholic Times.* Full of chivalry and knightly deeds, not unmixed with touches of quaint humour."—*Court Journal.* "A graceful and pleasing collection of stories."—*Daily News.* "There is a high purpose in this charming book, one which is steadily pursued—it is the setting forth of the true meaning of chivalry."—*Morning Post.*

A Daughter of St. Dominic. By Grace Ramsay (Kathleen O'Meara). 1s. 6d.

"A beautiful little work. The narrative is highly interesting."—*Dublin Review.* "It is full of courage and faith and Catholic heroism."—*Universe.* "A beautiful picture of the wonders effected by ubiquitous charity, and still more by fervent prayer."—*Tablet.*

Spirit of St. John the Baptist. 1s.

Annals of the Holy Childhood. 3d.

The Angels and the Sacraments.—Stories for my Children. 1s.

Stories from many Lands. By E. L. Hervey. 3s. 6d.

"Very well and, above all, very briefly told. The stories are short and varied. The Godmother's Anecdotes are very good stories."—*Saturday Review.* "A great number of short Stories and Anecdotes of a good moral tone."—*Tablet.* "A delightful fairy Godmother is this, who promises to rival the famous Princess Scheherezade as a story-teller."—*Weekly Register.* "Suitable for boys and girls of ten or twelve years, and is capable of teaching them not a few wholesome truths in an agreeable but really impressive manner."—*Illustrated London News.* "A charming collection of tales, illustrating some great truths."—*Church Times.* "With a few exceptions each story has 'some heart of meaning in it,' and tends to kindle in the mind all that is good and noble."—*Windsor Gazette.* "A collection of short stories, anecdotes, and apologues on various topics, delightfully told."—*Athenæum.*

Bessy; or the Fatal Consequence of Telling Lies. By Miss K. M. Weld. 1s.

"This is a very good tale to put into the hands of young servants."—*Tablet.* "The moral teaching is of course thoroughly Catholic, and conveyed in a form extremely interesting."—*Weekly Register.*

Kainer; or, the Usurer's Doom. By the Author of "Industry and Laziness." 1s.

"A very tastefully printed book, and the translation is clear and tasteful—well done, in fact."—*Irish Monthly.*

Tom's Crucifix, and other Tales. By M. F. S. 3s.6d.; or separately, 1s. each.

Tom's Crucifix, and Pat's Rosary.
Good for Evil, and Joe Ryan's Repentance.
The Old Prayer Book, and Charlie Pearson's Medal.
Catherine's Promise, and Norah's Temptation.
Annie's First Prayer, and Only a Picture.

"Simple stories for the use of teachers of Christian doctrine."—*Universe.* "This is a volume of short, plain, and simple stories, written with the view of illustrating the Catholic religion practically by putting Catholic practices in an interesting light before the mental eyes of children. The whole of the tales in the volume before us are exceedingly well written."—*Weekly Register.*

Ora pro Nobis; or, Tristram's Friends. By Rev. F. Drew. 1s.

Fluffy. A Tale for Boys. By M. F. S., author of "Tom's Crucifix and other Tales." 3s.

" A charming little story. The narrative is as wholesome through out as a breath of fresh air, and as beautiful in the spirit of it as a beam of moonlight."—*Weekly Register.* "The tale is well told. We cannot help feeling an interest in the fortunes of Fluffy."—*Tablet.*

The Three Wishes. A Tale. By M. F. S. 2s.

" A pretty neatly told story for girls. There is much quiet pathos in it and a warm Catholic spirit."—*The Month.* " We are glad to welcome this addition to the story-books for which the author is already favourably known."—*United Irishman.* "The tale is singularly interesting. The story of Gertrude with her gratified wish has about it all the interest of a romance, and will, no doubt, find especial favour."—*Weekly Register.* " Like everything which M. F. S. writes, the book is full of interest."—*Tablet.* The chief neroine is a striking model of what a young woman ought to be, and may become, if animated by sincere desire."—*Catholic Times.*

Catherine Hamilton. A Tale. By M. F. S. 1s. 6d.

" We have no doubt this will prove a very attractive book to the little folks, and would be glad to see it widely circulated."—*Catholic World.* " A short, simple, and well-told story, illustrative of the power of grace to correct bad temper in a wayward girl."—*Weekly Register.* "We are very much pleased with this little book."—*Tablet.*

Catherine grown Older. By M. F. S. 2s.

" Those who are familiar with the history of Catherine in her wayward childhood will welcome with no little satisfaction this sequel to her story from the hand of the same charming writer. There is a simplicity about the style and an earnest tenderness in the manner of the narrative which renders it singularly impressive." —*Weekly Register.* " Catherine's character will delight English children."—*Tablet.*

The two volumes in one, 3s.

Terry O'Flinn. By the Very Rev. Dr. Tandy. 2s.

" The writer possesses considerable literary power."—*Register.* "A most singular production."—*Universe.* " An unpretending yet a very touching story."—*Waterford News.* "Excellent indeed is the idea of embodying into a story the belief that there is ever beside us a guardian angel who reads the thoughts of our hearts and strives to turn us to good."—*Catholic World.* " The idea is well sustained throughout."—*Church Times.*

The Adventures of a Protestant in Search of a Religion: being the Story of a late Student of Divinity at Bunyan Baptist College; a Nonconformist Minister, who seceded to the Catholic Church. By Iota. 3s. 6d.; cheap edition, 2s.

"Will well repay its perusal."—*Universe.* "This precious volume."—*Baptist.* "No one will deny 'Iota' the merit of entire originality."—*Civilian.* "A valuable addition to every Catholic library.' *Tablet.* "There is much cleverness in it."—*Nonconformist.* "Malicious and wicked."—*English Independent.* "An admirable and amusing, yet truthful and genuinely sparkling work. The characters are from life."—*Catholic Opinion.*

The Village Lily. Fcap. 8vo. 1s.

"Charming little story."—*Weekly Register.*

Rosalie; or, the Memoirs of a French Child. Written by herself. 1s. 6d.

"It is prettily told, and in a natural manner. The account of Rosalie's illness and First Communion is very well related. We can recommend the book for the reading of children."—*Tablet.* "The tenth chapter is beautiful."—*Universe.* "The lessons inculcated tend to improve the youthful mind. We cannot too strongly recommend the book."—*Waterford News.* "This is one of those nicely written stories for children which we now and then come across."—*Catholic World.* "Charmingly written."—*Church Herald.*

The Story of Marie and other Tales. 2s. 6d.

"A very nice little collection of stories, thoroughly Catholic in their teaching."—*Tablet.* "A series of short pretty stories, told with much simplicity."—*Universe.* "A number of short pretty stories, replete with religious teaching, told in simple language."—*Weekly Register.*

The Mission Cross. An Abstinence Tale. By Mrs. Bartle Teeling, author of "Roman Violets," and "The Violet Sellers—a Drama." 1s. 6d.

Sir Ælfric and other Tales. By the Rev. G. Bampfield. 18mo. 6d.; cloth, 1s.

The Last of the Catholic O'Malleys. A Tale. By M. Taunton.

"A sad and stirring tale, simply written, and sure to secure for itself readers."—*Tablet.* "Deeply interesting. It is well adapted for parochial and school libraries."—*Weekly Register.* "A very pleasing tale."—*The Month.* "Simply and naturally told."—*Freeman's Journal.*

My Lady at Last. A Tale. By M. Taunton, author of "The Last of the Catholic O'Malleys." 3s. 6d.

Clare's Sacrifice. An impressive little tale, for First Communicants. By C. M. O'Hara. 6d.

Agnes Wilmott's History, and the Lessons it Taught. By M. A. Pennell, author of "Bertram Eldon," "Nellie Gordon," &c. 1s. 6d.

Killed at Sedan. A Novel. By Samuel Richardson, A.B., B.L., of the Middle Temple. 5s.

Eagle and Dove. From the French of Zénaide Fleuriot, by Emily Bowles. 3s. 6d.

"We recommend our readers to peruse this well-written story."—*Register.* " One of the very best stories we have ever dipped into." —*Church Times.* "Admirable in tone and purpose."—*Church Herald.* " A real gain. It possesses merits far above the pretty fictions got up by English writers."—*Dublin Review.* " There is an air of truth and sobriety about this little volume, nor is there any attempt at sensation."—*Tablet.*

Legends of the 13th Century. By the Rev. Henry Collins. 3s.

" A casket of jewels. Most fascinating as legends and none the less profitable for example, consolation, and encouragement."— *Weekly Register.* " The legends are full of deep spiritual teaching, and they are almost all authenticated."—*Tablet.* " Well translated and beautifully got up."—*The Month.* " Full of heavenly wisdom," —*Catholic Opinion.* " The volume reminds us forcibly of Rodriguez's ' Christian Perfection.'"—*Dublin Review.*

Little Books of St. Nicholas. Tales for Children. By Rev. F. Drew. 1s. each.

1. Oremus ; 2. Dominus Vobiscum ; 3. Pater Noster ; 4. Per Jesum Christum ; 5. Veni Creator ; 6. Credo ; 7. Ave Maria ; 8. Ora pro nobis ; 9. Corpus Christi ; 10. Dei Genitrix ; 11. Requiem ; 12. Miserere ; 13. Deo Gratias ; 14. Guardian Angel. [Numbers 1 to 8 are ready.]

Chats about the Rosary; or, Aunt Margaret's Little Neighbours. By Miss Plues. Fcap. 8vo. 3s.

" There is scarcely any devotion so calculated as the Rosary to keep up a taste for piety in little children, and we must be grateful for any help in applying its lessons to the daily life of those who already love it in their unconscious tribute to its value and beauty." —*Month.* " We do not know of a better book for reading aloud to children, it will teach them to understand and to love the Rosary."— *Tablet.* Illustrative of each of the mysteries, and connecting each with the practice of some particular virtue."—*Catholic Opinion.* "This pretty book carries out a very good idea, much wanted, to impress upon people who do not read much the vivid picture or story of each mystery of the Rosary."—*Dublin Review.*

The Rose of Venice. A Venetian Tale. By S. Christopher. Crown 8vo., 3s. 6d.

"A very interesting and well-told story."—*The Month*.

Margarethe Verflassen. Translated from the German by Mrs. Smith Sligo. 3s.

"A portrait of a very holy and noble soul, whose life was passed in constant practical acts of the love of God."—*Weekly Register*. "It is the picture of a true woman's life, well fitted up with the practice of ascetic devotion and loving unwearied activity about all the works of mercy."—*Tablet*. "Those who may wish to know something about Convent life will find it faithfully pourtrayed in every important particular in the volume before us. We cordially commend it to our readers."—*Northern Star*.

Sir Thomas Maxwell and his Ward. By Miss Bridges. Fcap. 8vo. 1s. 6d.

Adolphus; or, the Good Son. 18mo. gilt, 6d.

Nicholas; or, the Reward of a Good Action. 6d.

The Lost Children of Mount St. Bernard. Gilt, 6d.

The Baker's Boy; or, the Results of Industry. 6d.

A Broken Chain. 18mo. gilt, 6d.

Cardinal Wolsey. By Agnes Stewart. 6s.

Margaret Roper. By the same author. 6s.

Cardinal Pole. By the same author. 7s. 6d., gilt, 10s.

Earl Nugent's Daughter. By the same author. 5s.

Sir Thomas More. By the same author. 7s., gilt, 9s.

The Yorkshire Plot. By the same author. 6s.

Bishop Fisher. By the same author. 7s.

The Catholic "Pilgrim's Progress"—The Journey of Sophia and Eulalie to the Palace of True Happiness. Translated by the Rev. Father Bradbury, Mount St. Bernard's. 2s. 6d.

"The book is essentially suited to women, and especially to those who purpose devoting themselves to the hidden life of sanctity. It will prove, however, a useful gift to many young ladies whose lot is in the world."—*Weekly Register.* "This mode of teaching imparts an extraordinary degree of vividness and reality."—*Church Review.* "Unquestionably the book is one that for a certain class of minds will have a great charm."—*The Scotsman.* "No one can weary with the perusal, and most people will enjoy it very much."—*Tablet.*

Diary of a Confessor of the Faith. 12mo., 1s.

Nellie Gordon, the Factory Girl; or Lost and Saved. By M. A. Pennell. 6d.

Tim O'Halloran's Choice; or, From Killarney to New York. By Sister M. F. Clare. 3s. 6d.

Legends of the Saints. By M. F. S., author of "Stories of the Saints." 3s. 6d.

"A pretty little book, couched in studiously simple language."—*Church Times.* "A number of short legends, told in simple language for young readers by one who has already given us two charming volumes of 'Stories of the Saints.'"—*Tablet.* "Here we have more than fifty tales, told with singular taste, and ranging over a vast geographical area. Not one of them will be passed over by the reader."—*Catholic Times.* "A delightful boon for youthful readers."—*Weekly Register.* "It is got up in the most attractive as well as substantial style as regards binding, paper, and typography, while the simple and beautiful legends are told in a graceful and flowing manner, which cannot fail to rivet the attention and interest of the youthful reader."—*United Irishman.*

Stories of the Saints. By M. F. S. 1st Series, 3s. 6d., 2nd Series, 3s. 6d. 3rd Series, 3s. 6d. 4th Series, 3s. 6d. 5th Series, 3s. 6d.

"As lovely a little book as we have seen for many a day."—*Weekly Register.* "Interesting not only for children but for persons of every age and degree."—*Tablet.* "A great desideratum. Very pleasantly written."—*The Month.* "A very attractive volume. A delightful book."—*Union Review.* "Admirably adapted for reading aloud to children, or for their own private reading."—*Catholic Opinion.* "Being full of anecdotes, they are especially attractive."—*Church Herald.* "Well selected."—*Dublin Review.*

Stories of Holy Lives. By M. F. S. Fcp. 8vo., 3s. 6d.

"The stories seem well put together."—*The Month.* "It sets before us clearly and in simple language the most striking features in the character and history of many whose very names are dear to the hearts of Catholics."—*Tablet.*

Stories of Martyr Priests. By M. F. S. 12mo., 3s. 6d.

"The stories are written with the utmost simplicity, and with such an earnest air of reality about every page that the youthful reader may forget that he has a book in his hand, and can believe that he is 'listening to a story.'"—*Weekly Register.* "It has been the task of the writer, while adhering strictly to historical facts, to present the lives of these Christian heroes in a pleasing and attractive form, so that, while laying before the youthful minds deeds as thrilling as any to be found in the pages of romance, a chapter in her history is laid open which is at once the glory and the shame of England."—*United Irishman.* "Short memoirs well written and which cannot fail to attract not only 'the Catholic Boys of England,' to whom the book is dedicated, but also all the men and women of England to whom the Catholic faith is dear."—*Tablet.* "Sad stories of over thirty Priests who perished for conscience sake."—*Catholic Times.* "No lives of great men can depict so glorious a picture as these Stories of Martyred Priests, and we trust they will be read far and wide."—*Dublin Review.*

The Story of the Life of St. Paul. By M. F. S., author of "Legends of the Saints," &c. 2s.

"A most attractive theme for the prolific pen of the author of 'Tom's Crucifix and other Tales.'"—*Weekly Register.* "The author knew instinctively how to present the incidents most effectively, and has made the most of them."—*Catholic Times.*

Bible Stories from the Old Testament. Twelve Stories of the Jewish Church, to interest the young in the fortunes of God's ancient Church, by throwing the Scripture narrative into a slightly different form. By Charles Walker. 2s.

' CONTENTS :—The Sacrifice of Abel.—The Ship of Safety.—The City of Confusion.—Melchisedech, King of Salem.—The Sabbath Breaker.—Achan.—The Child Prophet of Silo.—The Building of the Temple.—The Altar at Beth-El.—The Repentance of Nineve.—The Furnace of Babylon.—The Prophecy of Malachias.

Life of St. Wenefred, Virgin Martyr and Abbess, Patroness of North Wales and Shrewsbury. By Rev. T. Meyrick, M.A. With Frontispiece, 2s.

Albertus Magnus: his Life and Scholastic Labours. From original Documents. By Professor Sighart. Translated by Rev. Fr. T. A. Dixon, O.P. 8vo., 6s.

"A translation of Dr. Sighart's 'Albertus Magnus' will be welcome in many quarters. The volume is admirably printed and beautifully got up, and the frontispiece is a valuable engraving of B. Albert's portrait after Fiesole."—*Dublin Review.* "Albert the Great is not well known . . . yet he is one of those pioneers of inductive philosophy whom our modern men of science cannot without black ingratitude forget. His memory should be dear not only to those who value the sanctity of life, but to those also who try, as he did, to wrest from nature the reason of her doings."—*The Month.* "The volume is a large one, as befits the subject, and it carries the reader through most of the scenes of Albert's life with a graphic power . . . We recommend this book as worthy a place in every library."—*Catholic Times.* "The fullest record that has ever been penned of one of the grandest luminaries in the history of the Church."—*Weekly Register.* "The book is extremely interesting, full of information, and displays great power of research and critical judgment. . . . The volume is eminently worth perusal."—*Tablet.* "One of the most interesting religious biographies recently issued from the Catholic press."—*Irish Monthly.*

Lives of the First Religious of the Visitation of Holy Mary. By Mother Frances Magdalen de Chaugy. 2 vols., 10s. :—or separately :—

Life of Mother Marie Jacqueline Favre, Mother Jeanne Charlotte de Bréchard, Mother Peronne Marie de Châtel, Mother Claude Agnes Joli de la Roche. 6s.

Life of Sister Claude Simplicienne Fardel, Sister Marie Aimée de Chantal, Sister Françoise Gabrielle Bally, Sister Marie Denise de Martignat, Sister Anne Jacqueline Coste, Sister Marie Péronne Pernet, Sister Marie Séraphique de Chamflours. 6s.

S. Vincent Ferrer, his Life, Spiritual Teaching, and practical Devotion. By Fr. Pradel. Translated by Rev. Fr. Dixon, O.P. 5s.

Life of S. Bernardine of Siena. 5s.

Life of S. Philip Benizi. 5s.

Life of S. Veronica Giuliani, and Blessed Battista Varani. 5s.

Life of S. John of God. 5s.

The Lives of the Early Popes. St. Peter to Charlemagne. By Rev. Thomas Meyrick, M.A. 8vo. 6s.

Life of B. Giovanni Colombini. By Feo Belcari. Translated from the editions of 1541 and 1832. Cr. 8vo. 3s. 6d.

Sketch of the Life and Letters of the Countess Adelstan. By E. A. M., author of "Rosalie, or the Memoirs of a French Child," "Life of Paul Seigneret," &c. 2s.

"The great interest of the book, even above the story of the conversion of her husband, is the question of education. The essay on the bringing up of children and the comparative merits and demerits of Convent and home education, is well worth the careful study both of parents and those entrusted with the task of instruction."—*The Month.* "Her judgments are always wise."—*Catholic Opinion.* "We can safely recommend this excellent little biographical sketch. It offers no exciting interest, but it is calculated to edify all."—*Tablet.*

Life of Paul Seigneret, Seminarist of Saint-Sulpice. 1s. 6d.

"An affecting and well-told narrative... It will be a great favourite, especially with our pure-minded, high-spirited young people."—*Universe.* "We commend it to parents with sons under their care, and especially do we recommend it to those who are charged with the education and training of our Catholic youth."—*Register.*

Inner Life of Père Lacordaire. By Père Chocarne. Translated by Augusta Theodosia Drane. 6s. 6d.

Life of Sister Mary Cherubina Clare of S. Francis. With Preface by Lady Herbert.

Life of Gregory Lopez, the Hermit. By Canon Doyle, O.S.B. 12mo., 3s. 6d.

St. Angela Merici. Her Life, her Virtues, and her Institute. 12mo., 3s.

Life of St. Columba, &c. By M. F. Cusack. 8vo., 6s.

Recollections of Cardinal Wiseman, &c. By M. J. Arnold. 2s.

Lives of the Saints, from Alban Butler. Selected and edited by Right Rev. Mgr. Goddard. 5s.

Life of St. Mildred, Abbess of Minster in Thanet. By a Lay-Tertiary of St. Francis. 2s

Life of Rev. Fr. Hermann (Discalced Carmelite). From the French of the Abbé Charles Sylvani. By Mrs. Raymond-Barker. 3s. 6d. and 4s. 6d.

Life and Miracles of St. Benedict. From St. Gregory the Great, by Rev. Dom E. J. Luck. fcap. 8vo., 1s. ; stronger bound, 2s.

Life of St. Boniface. By Mrs. Hope. 6s.

Life of Fr. Benvenuto Bambozzi, O.M.C., of the Conventual Friars Minor. Translated from the Italian of Fr. Nicholas Treggiari, D.D. 3s. 6d.

Life of the Ven. Anna Maria Taigi. From the French of Calixte, by A. V. Smith Sligo. 3s. 6d.

Life of Father Mathew. By Sister Mary Francis Clare. 2s. 6d.

Life of St. Patrick. 12mo. 1s. ; 8vo. 10s., gilt.

Life of St. Bridget, and of other Saints of Ireland. 1s.

Life, Passion, Death, and Resurrection of Our Blessed Lord. Translated from Ribadeneira. 1s.

Life of S. Edmund of Canterbury. 1s. and 1s. 6d.

Life of St. Francis of Assisi. From St. Bonaventure. By Miss Lockhart. 3s. 6d.

Pius IX. From his Birth to his Death. By G. White. 6d.

Life of the Ever-Blessed Virgin. 1s.

Our Blessed Lady of Lourdes: a Faithful Narrative of the Apparitions of the Blessed Virgin. By F. C. Husenbeth, D.D., 6d.; with Novena to Our Lady of Lourdes, cloth, 1s. Novena, separately, 4d.; Litany, 1d., or 6s. per 100. Medal, 1d.

A Month at Lourdes and its Neighbourhood in the Summer of 1877. By Hugh Caraher. Two Illustrations, 2s.

Life of the Ven. Elizabeth Canori Mora. From the Italian, with Preface by Lady Herbert 3s. 6d.

The History of the Italian Revolution. The Revolution of the Barricades. (1796—1849.) By the Chevalier O'Clery, M.P., K.S.G. 8vo. 4s.

To Rome and Back. Fly-leaves from a Flying Tour. Edited by W. H. Anderdon, S.J. 12mo., 2s.

"Graphic and vigorous sketches. As Father Anderdon says, Truly they have their special interest, by reason of date no less than of place and scene. 'To Rome and Back' refers to Rome and back at the time of the Papal Jubilee. It is as beautiful a celebration of that memorable event as has anywhere appeared."—*Weekly Register*. "We note in the Authoress a power of condensing a description in a bold and striking metaphor. There is all a woman's quickness and keenness of perception, and a power of sympathy with the noble, the beautiful, and the true."—*The Month*. "A charming book. . . . Besides pleasant description, there is evidence of much thought in parts of the book."—*Dublin Review*.

The First Apostles of Europe. The 2nd Edition of "The Conversion of the Teutonic Race." By Mrs. Hope. 2 vols. crown 8vo. The Life of St. Boniface can now only be had. 6s.

"Mrs. Hope has quite grasped the general character of the Teutonic nations and their true position with regard to Rome and the world in general... It is a great thing to find a writer of a book of this class so clearly grasping and so boldly setting forth truths, which familiar as they are to scholars, are still utterly unknown—or worse than unknown, utterly misconceived—by most of the writers of our smaller literature."—*Saturday Review*. "A brilliant and compact history of the Germans, Franks, and the various tribes of the former Jutes, Angles, and Saxons, who jointly formed the Anglo-Saxon, or, more correctly, English people. . . . Many of the episodes and notices of the Apostolic Missionaries, as well as the general story, are very happily and gracefully conveyed.'—*Northern Star*. "This is a real addition to our Catholic literature."—*Tablet*.

Holy Places; their Sanctity and Authenticity. By the Rev. Fr. Philpin. With Maps. Crown 8vo. 3s. 6d.; cheap edition, 2s.6d.

"Fr. Philpin weighs the comparative value of extraordinary, ordinary, and natural evidence, and gives an admirable summary of the witness of the early centuries regarding the holy places of Jerusalem, with archæological and architectural proofs. It is a complete treatise of the subject."—*Month.* "The author treats his subject with a thorough system, and a competent knowledge."—*Church Herald.*

Flowers of Christian Wisdom: Selections from various well-known authors on the following subjects—Man and his Soul; The Christian; Human Respect; Faith; The Church; The Last Things; Principles, Duties, and some Rules of Conduct; Duties towards God, His Name, His Day, His Ministers; The Fatherland and the Good Citizen; Duties towards Parents; Duty towards our Neighbour; Charity for the Poor; Friendships—Friends; True Honour; True Happiness; Innocence; Virtue; On Bad Passions; After a Fault; Holy Communion; Idleness and Work; On Reading—Good, Bad, and Frivolous Books; The Service of God—True Piety; On Religion or Devotion; Of Faults—of Little Faults; Of Vanity and Pride; Mildness; Amenity, Politeness, Conversations, Liberty; The Dwelling, Clothing, Food; The Theatre, Balls, Gaming; On Adversity; A Sketch of a Plan of Life. Compiled by Lucien Henry, with Preface by Lady Herbert of Lea. 1s. 6d.

"There are so many books, that one cannot even read all those that are excellent; why then lose time in turning over the leaves of those that are spoilt by the evil spirit ?"—*Lacordaire.*

BY ARTHUR AND T. W. M. MARSHALL.

Comedy of Convocation in the English Church. Edited by Archdeacon Chasuble, D.D. 2s. 6d.

The Oxford Undergraduate of Twenty Years Ago: his Religion, his Studies, his Antics. By a Bachelor of Arts. 2s. 6d.

"The writing is full of brilliancy and point."—*Tablet.* "It will deservedly attract attention, not only by the briskness and liveliness of its style, but also by the accuracy of the picture which it probably gives of an individual experience."—*The Month.*

The Harmony of Anglicanism. Report of a Conference on Church Defence. 2s. 6d.

"'Church Defence' is characterised by the same caustic irony, the same good-natured satire, the same logical acuteness which distinguished its predecessor, the 'Comedy of Convocation.' . . . A more scathing bit of irony we have seldom met with."—*Tablet.*
"Clever, humorous, witty, learned, written by a keen but sarcastic observer of the Establishment, it is calculated to make defenders wince as much as it is to make all others smile."—*Nonconformist.*

Dramas, Comedies, Farces. (*See* also page 26.)

Mary, Queen of Scots.   Tragedy in Three Acts. *Mixed.* 6d.

Bluebeard; or, the Key of the Cellar.   Drama in Three Acts. *Children.* 6d.

The Violet Sellers. Drama in Three Acts. *Children.* 6d.

Whittington and his Cat.   Drama in Nine Scenes. *Children.* 6d.

St. Eustace. A Drama in Five Acts. *Male.* 6d.

St. William of York. A Drama in Two Acts. *Male.* 6d.

He would be a Lord.   Comedy in Three Acts. *Male.* 2s.

The Enchanted Violin.   Comedy in Two Acts. *Male.* 6d.

Shandy Maguire. A Farce in Two Acts. *Male.* 6d.

The Duchess Transformed.   A Comedy in One Act. By W. H. A. *Female.* 6d.

The Reverse of the Medal.   A Drama in Four Acts. *Female.* 6d.

Ernscliff Hall; or, Two Days spent with a Great Aunt. A Drama in Three Acts. *Female.* 6d.

Filiola. A Drama in Four Acts. *Female.* 6d.

The Secret. Drama in One Act. *Female.* 6d.

The Convert Martyr; or, Dr. Newman's "Callista," dramatised by Dr. Husenbeth. 1s.

R. WASHBOURNE'S
Catalogue of Books from America.

All these prices are *nett* (no reduction).

" Words in Italic thus (*Friendly*) signify that the book is a section of the one referred to in Italic.

Adventures of a Captain. By Lady Blanche Murphy ...	2	6
Adventures of a Casquet, The	2	0
African Fabiola	5	0
Alba's Dream, and other Stories	5	0
Alice Harmon, and other Tales. By an "Exile of Erin" ...	5	0
Alice Riordan, the Blind Man's Daughter	3	0
All for Love; or, from the Manger to the Cross	7	0
Alzog's Church History. 3 vols.	60	0
Angel Guide; or, Year of First Communion	3	0
Anthony; or, the Silver Crucifix	2	0
Apostleship of Prayer. By Rev. H. Ramière	4	0
Apostolic, An, Woman; Sister Francis Xavier	8	0
Appeal, An, and a Defiance. By Cardinal Deschamps ...	2	0
Assunta Howard, and other Stories and Sketches... ...	5	0
Aurelia; or, The Jews of Capena Gate. By Quinton ...	5	0
Barbara Leigh. A Christmas Sketch. By A. L. S. ...	3	0
Beauties of the Catholic Church. By Fr. Shadlier ...	7	0
Bellecius' Triduum and Spiritual Conferences	3	0
Benedict's (St.) Manual. By Rev. Fr. Meyer, O.S.B. ...	5	0
Bertha; or, The Consequence of a Fault. 2s. and ...	3	0
Better Part, The. A Tale from Real Life	2	0
Bible. Large 4to., morocco elegant, with clasp	72	0
Bible. 4to., cloth, 21s.; French morocco, 27s. 6d.; morocco	34	0
Bible. 18mo., cloth, 6s.; roan, 7s.; persian calf, 9s.; morocco, 12s.; extra gilt	14	0
Bible History for the Use of Catholic Schools. By a Teacher. Illustrated	4	0
Bible History for the Use of Schools. By Bishop Gilmour. Illustrated	2	0
Blanche de Marsilly. An Episode of the Revolution ...	2	0
Blessed Virgin, Life of the. By Bishop Dupanloup ...	10	0
Blind Friend of the Poor. Mgr. de Segur	2	0
Book of the Professed. By author of "Golden Sands" ...	4	0
Burke's Sermons and Lectures. 3 vols.	26	0
Butler's Lives of the Saints. 4 vols., 32s.; gilt 36s.; or, bound in 2 vols., 24s.; gilt	28	0
See **Lives of the Saints**		
Cahill's Sermons and Lectures	8	0
Captain Rougemont; or, the Miraculous Conversion ...	2	0
Cassilda; or, The Moorish Princess of Toledo	2	0

R. Washbourne's American Publications (nett). 21

Catherine (St.) of Genoa, Life ...	4	0
Catholic Keepsake. A Gift Book for all Seasons ...	3	0
Catholic Priest and Scientists. By Rev. J. W. Vahey ...	8	0
Catholicity in the Carolinas and Georgia. By Fr. O'Connell	10	0
Christ in His Church; Busingen's Church History, translated by Rev. R. Brennan. Illustrated ...	8	0
Christian Life and Vocation. By Rev. J. Berthier ...	4	0
Christian Father. From the German of Rev. W. Cramer. 1s. paper ...	2	0
Christian Mother. Ditto, same prices.		
Christian Truths. Lectures by Rt. Rev. Bishop Chatard	5	0
Christmas for our dear Little Ones, The First. Illustrated	5	0
Church and Moral World. By Rev. A. J. Thébaud, S.J. ...	12	0
Church and the Gentile World. By the same. 3 vols. ...	24	0
Church History. 1 By Alzog, 3 vols., 60s. 2 By Darras, 4 vols., 40s. 3 By Busingen, 8s. 4 By Brennan, 4s. 5 By Noethen, 6s.		
Commandments of God. By Rev. M. Müller ...	8	0
Communion, Holy. By Hubert Lebon ...	3	0
Conscience's Works: Amulet and Poor Gentleman, 4s.; Conscript, Blind Rosa, and The Miser, 4s.; Count Hugo and Curse of the Village 4s.; Happiness of Being Rich, Ricketicketack, Wooden Clara, 4s.; Ludovic and Gertrude, Young Doctor, 4s.; Merchant of Antwerp, 5s.; Lion of Flanders, 4s.; Veva, 4s.; Village Innkeeper and Fisherman's Daughter, 4s.		
Convert, The: Leaves from My Experience. By Brownson	6	0
Counsels for each Day in the Week (*Friendly*) ...	0	6
Counsels of a Catholic Mother to her Daughter ...	2	0
Crasset's Devout Meditations ...	6	0
Crown of Heaven, The. From the German of Stoeger ...	5	0
Crown of Thorns, Mystery of. By a Passionist Father ...	4	0
Dalaradia; or, The Days of King Milcho. By W. Collins	3	0
Darras's Church History. 4 vols. ...	40	0
Dignity, Authority, and Duties of Parents. By Rev. M. Müller ...	9	0
Divine Paraclete. Sermons. By Rev. T. S. Preston ...	4	0
Divine Sanctuary, The. By the Rev. T. S. Preston ...	4	0
Divinity of Christ, The. By Rt. Rev. Dr. Rosecrans ...	2	0
Dumb Boy ...	2	6
Dupont (Léon Papin-) Life of (*Holy Man of Tours*) ...	5	0
Ecclesiastical Law, Elements of. By Rev. S. B. Smith, D.D.	16	0
,, ,, Vol. 2, Ecclesiastical Trials ...	16	0
Eliane. By Mrs. Craven ...	4	0

R. Washbourne's American Publications (nett).

Emerald Gems. Irish Fireside Tales	5 0
Epistles and Gospels, Explanation of. By Goffine ...	8 0
Ethel Hamilton. By Anna T. Sadlier	3 0
Eucharist, (Blessed) our Greatest Treasure. By Rev. M. Muller	5 0
Eucharist (Holy) and Penance. By Rev. M. Müller ...	7 0
Eugenie de Guerin's Letters	6 0
European Civilisation, Protestantism and Catholicity Compared. By Balmes	10 0
Evidences of Catholicity. By Archbishop Spalding ...	8 0
Faith of Our Fathers, The. By Rev. Archbishop Gibbons	4 0
Cheap edition, in paper covers, 2s.	
Father Oswald. A Genuine Catholic Story	3 0
Pickle Fortune. A Story of Place La Grève	3 0
First Communicants, Instructions for. By Dr. Schmitt ...	2 6
First Communion (My). From the German of Fr. Buchmann	3 0
First Communion, Year of. (*Angel Guide*)	3 0
Fisherman's Daughter. Translated by Mrs. Monroe, 2s. and	3 0
Four Seasons, The. By Rev. J. W. Vahey	3 0
Francis' (St.) Manual for Members of Third Order. 824 pp.	3 0
Francis of Sales (St.), Maxims of, for every day ...	2 0
Francis of Sales (St.), New Year Greetings	1 0
Francis Xavier (St.), Life of. From the Italian of Bartoli	6 0
Friendly Voice; or, the Daily Monitor	0 6
Future of Catholic Peoples. By Baron de Haulleville ...	5 0
Genius of Christianity. By Chateaubriand	8 0
Gertrude (St.) Manual; or Spirit of Devotion, 504 pages ...	4 0
God the Teacher of Mankind. By Rev. M. Müller:	
Holy Eucharist and Penance	7 0
The Greatest and the First Commandment	8 0
Precepts of the Church	7 0
Dignity, Authority, and Duties of Parents	9 0
Sacramentals, Prayer, Vices and Virtues, Perfection, etc.	7 0
Good Thoughts for Priest and People; or, Short Meditations for Every Day in the Year. By Rev. T. Noethan ...	6 0
Goffine's Epistles and Gospels	8 0
Golden Sands. First and Second Series, each, 4s.; Third Series	3 0
Governess, The; or, The Effects of Good Example. By G. H. Miles	3 0
Great-Grandmother's Secret, The. 2s. superior edition ...	3 0
Gretchen's Gift; or, A Noble Sacrifice. By A. I. S. ...	3 0
Guardian Angel, Memoirs of a. By the Abbé Chardon ...	3 0
Hill's Elements of Philosophy. 2 vols.	12 0
History, Compendium of. By Kerney	5 0
Hofbauer (Fr. Clement), Life of, in English. By Lady Herbert	5 0

R. Washbourne's American Publications (nett). 23

Holy Man of Tours; or, the Life of Léon Papin-Dupont	5	0
Household Science. By author of "Golden Sands"	3	0
Idols; or, The Secret of the Rue Chaussée d'Antin	5	0
Indian Sketches. By Rev. P. J. De Smet, S.J.	2	0
Ingersoll, Notes on. By Rev. A Lambert	2	0
Intellectual Philosophy. By Rev. J. De Concilio	5	0
Invitation Heeded. By James Kent Stone	5	0
Ireland, Past and Present. By D. P. Conyngham	12	0
Irish Faith in America. Recollections of a Missionary	3	0
Irish Fireside Tales (*Emerald*)...	5	0
Irish Martyrs and Confessors, Lives of. By Myles O'Reilly	10	0
Irish Race (The) Past and the Present. By Fr. Thébaud	10	0
Joint Venture, The; a Tale in Two Lands	4	0
Kerney's Compendium of History	5	0
King's Page, The, and other Stories. By Anna T. Sadlier	3	0
Knowledge and Love of Jesus Christ. St. Jure, 3 vols.	24	0
Lacordaire's Conferences: Life	6	0
Lacordaire's Letters to Young Men	6	0
Lenten Sermons. By Fr. Segneri. 2 vols.	10	0
Le Gras (Mdlle.), Life of, Foundress of the Sisters of Charity	6	0
LEO XIII., Life and Acts of. With a Sketch of the Last Days of Pius IX. Edited by Rev. J. E. Keller, S.J. Illustrated	8	0
Leper's Son	2	0
Letters of a Young Irishwoman to her Sister	5	0
Life of our Lord and the Blessed Virgin. By Rev. R. Brennan. Large 4to., illustrated, half-morocco	40	0
Liguori (St.) Life of	8	0
Literature, Student's Handbook By Rev. O. L. Jenkins	6	0
Little Lives of Great Saints	4	0
Little Rose of the Sacred Heart	2	0
Little Saint of Nine Years. From French of Mgr. de Segur	2	0
Little Treatise on the Little Virtues. By Fr. Roberti, S.J.	2	0
Little Treatise on Little Sufferings	1	0
Lives of the Deceased Bishops of the Catholic Church in the United States. By R. H. Clarke. 2 vols.	24	0
Lives of the Saints. By Butler. 4 vols., 8vo., 32s.; gilt, 36s.; or bound in 2 vols., 8vo., 24s.; gilt	28	0
Lives of the Saints, Pictorial, with Reflection for Every Day	14	0
Lives of Patron Saints. Illustrated (*Patron*)	10	0
Louisa Kirkbride. By Fr. Thébaud. Illustrated	6	0
Loretto; or, The Choice. By G. H. Miles	3	0
Maidens of Hallowed Names	4	0
Maddalena; The Orphan of the Via Media	3	0
Manual of the Sacred Thirst (to repress Intemperance)	2	6
Marcelle. A True Story. 2s., superior edition	3	0

24 R. Washbourne's American Publications (nett).

Margaret Mary (Blessed), Letters of (*Sacred Heart*)	2	0
Marriage, Sure Way to a Happy. By Fr. Taylor. 1s. 6d. paper	3	0
Mary, The Knowledge of. By Rev. J. de Concilio	5	0
Mary Magdalene (St.), Life of	2	0
Mass (The). History of. By Rev. J. O'Brien	6	0
Mass (The). The Holy Sacrifice for the Living and the Dead. By Michael Müller, C.SS.R.	8	0
Meditations, Devout. By Crasset. Translated by Dorsey	6	0
Meditations for Every Day. By Vercruysse. 2 vols.	16	0
Miraculous Conversion (*Captain*)	2	0
Monk's Pardon. Translated by Anna T. Sadlier	5	0
Monks of the West. By the Count de Montalembert. 2 vols.	22	0
Moorish Princess of Toledo (*Cassilda*)	2	0
More (Sir Thomas). By Mrs. Monroe	5	0
Muard, Life of Rev. M. J. B. By Rt. Rev. Dom Robot, O.S.B.	5	0
Mysterious Beggar	2	0
Names that Live in Catholic Hearts	4	0
Neptune, The, at the Golden Horn. Illustrated	4	0
New Year Greetings. By St. Francis de Sales	1	0
Noethen's Church History	6	0
Novices, Manual of. By Author of 'Golden Sands'	4	0
Novitiate, Souvenir of the	3	0
O'Mahony, The, Chief of the Comeraghs. A Tale of '98	5	0
Only a Waif. By R. A. Braendle (' Pips ')	3	0
Orphan of Alsace	2	0
Orphan of Moscow. By Mrs. Sadlier	3	●
Paradise of God : or, the Virtues of the Sacred Heart	3	0
Paradise on Earth	2	0
Pastoral Medicine. Capellmann. Trans. by Rev. W. Dassel	5	0
Patira. From the French of Raoul de Navery	5	0
Patron Saints. By E. A. Starr. Illustrated	10	0
Paulists' Sermons : Five Minutes, 1864, 1865, 1871, each	5	0
Pearl among the Virtues, The. By Rev. P. A. De Doss, S.J.	3	0
Pearl of Antioch. By Abbé Bayle	5	0
Perico the Sad ; or, the Alvareda Family, and other Stories	5	0
Philomena (St.), Life and Miracles of	2	0
Philosophy, Elements of, comprising Logic and General Principles of Metaphysics. By Rev. Fr. Hill, S.J.	6	0
Philosophy, Ethics, or Moral. By W. H. Hill, S.J.	6	0
Pius IX., Last Days of. By Rev. J. E. Keller, S.J.	8	0
Praxis Synodalis	3	0
Precepts of the Church. By Rev. M. Müller	7	0
Priest of Auvrigny, The, etc.	2	0
Protestant Reformation. By Archbishop Spalding	12	0
Protestant Reformation, &c. By Rev. T. S. Preston	4	0
Protestant and Catholic Civilisation Compared (*Future*)	5	0
Raphaela. By Mlle. Monniot	5	0
Ravignan (Fr.), S. J., Life of. By Fr. de Ponlevoy	12	0
Recluse, The	2	0
Religious, The. By Rev. J. B. St. Jure. 2 vols.	18	0
Repertorium Oratoris Sacri: Outlines of 600 Sermons. 4 vols.	42	0
Richard ; or, Devotion to the Stuarts, 2s. superior edition	3	0
Rosary, The, and the Five Scapulars. By Rev. M. Müller	5	0

R. Washbourne's American Publications (nett). 25

Sacramentals, Prayer, Vices and Virtues, Christian Perfection, etc. By Rev. M. Müller	7 0
Sacred Chant, Manual of. By Fr. Mohr	2 6
Sacred Heart: Devotions for the first Friday of every month. By Père Huguet	2 0
Sacred Heart, Devotions to. By Rev. S. Franco, S.J.	3 0
Sacred Heart, Devotions to (*Little Virtues*)	2 0
Sacred Heart, Hours with	2 0
Sacred Heart, Manual. By Fr. Schouppe	1 6
Sacred Heart, Pearls from the Casket of	2 0
Sacred Heart, Virtues of. By Père Boudreaux, S.J.	3 0
Sacred Heart, Year of: A Thought for every day	2 0
Sally Cavanagh. By J. C. Kickham	4 0
Sanctuary Boy's Illustrated Manual	5 0
Scapulars (Five), The Devotion of. By Rev. M. Müller	5 0
Sermons for Every Sunday, etc.: Catholic Pulpit	10 0
Sermons, Short, for Low Masses. By Rev. Fr. Schouppe	8 0
Sermons, Repertorium Oratoris Sacri. 4 vols.	42 0
Sermons. Divine Paraclete. By Rev. T. S. Preston	4 0
Sermons. By the Paulists, 1864, 1865, 1871. Five Minutes, each	5 0
Sermons and Lectures. By Father Burke, O.P. 3 vols.	26 0
Sermons, Lectures, and Discourses. By Bp. Spalding	5 0
Sermons, One Hundred Short. By Rev. Fr. Thomas	10 0
Sermons on Our Lord, the B.V.M., and Moral Subjects. By Cardinal Wiseman. 2 vols.	12 0
Sermons (53), Preached in the Albany County Penitentiary. By Rev. T. Noethen	6 0
Sermons, Lectures, &c., of Rev. Dr. D. W. Cahill	8 0
Sermons or Lectures. By B. Chatard (*Christian Truths*)	5 0
Seton, Mgr., Essays on various subjects, chiefly Roman	8 0
Seton, Mrs., Order of Sisters of Charity	6 0
Short Stories on Christian Doctrine	4 0
Signs and Ceremonies, Teaching Truth by. Illustrated	4 0
Sister Natalie. By Mrs. Craven	4 0
Sisters of Charity, Manual of	4 0
Six Sunny Months, and other Stories	5 0
Society of Jesus, History of. By Daurignac	6 0
Spalding's (Abp.) Works. 5 vols.	40 0
Cheap edition: Evidences of Catholicity, 8s. Miscellanea, 12s.; Protestant Reformation, 12s.	
Spiritual Man. By St. Jure	6 0
Spiritual Direction. By Author of 'Golden Sands'	3 0
Stray Leaves from a Passing Life, and other Stories	6 0
Teaching Truth by Signs and Ceremonies	4 0
Teresa (St.), Life of. By Abbé Marie Joseph	4 0
Teresa (St.), Thoughts of, for every day in the Year	2 0
Thalia; or, Arianism and the Council of Nice. An Historical Tale of the Fourth Century. By the Abbé A. Bayle	5 0
Theologia Moralis S. Alphonsi Compendium. Auctore A. Konings, C.SS.R. 21s. 6d. 2 vols. in 1, half-morocco	27 0
Thesaurus Biblicus; or, Handbook of Scripture Reference	15 0
Thomas Aquinas (St.) Life of	4 0
Thomas's One Hundred Short Sermons	10 0

26   *R. Washbourne's American Publications (nett).*

Truce of God. A Tale of the XI. Century. By Miles	3	0
True Men as We Need Them. By Rev. B. O'Reilly	10	0
Truths of Salvation. By Rev. J. Pergmayr, S.J.	4	0
Two Brothers	2	0
Vacation Days. By author of "Golden Sands"	4	0
Village Steeple, The. A Tale	2	0
Vincent's (St.) Manual	3	0
Visits to the Blessed Sacrament (*Friendly*)	0	6
Vows, Catechism of. By Cotel	1	6
Weninger's Conferences. 2 vols.	20	0
What Catholics do not Believe. By Bishop Ryan	1	0
Wiseman's (Cardinal) Essays. 6 vols.	30	0
Wiseman's (Cardinal) Sermons on Our Lord and B. V. M., and Moral Subjects. 2 vols. each	6	0
Woman of Culture. By J. T. Smith	5	0
Young Flower-Maker	2	0
Zita (St.), Life of	2	0
Vercruysse's Meditations for Every Day. 2 vols.	16	0

DRAMAS, etc.*

Babbler, The. A Drama in One Act. By Mrs. J. Sadlier. *Male*	1	6
Christmas Tree. Drama, One Act (*Mixed*)	1	6
Double Triumph, The. Dramatized from the Story of Placidus in the "Martyrs of the Coliseum." By Rev. A. J. O'Reilly. *Male*	2	6
Elder Brother, The. A Drama in Two Acts. By Mrs. J. Sadlier. *Male*	1	6
Fanny Allen, the First American Nun. A Drama in 5 Acts. *Female*	1	6
Invisible Hand, The. A Drama in Three Acts. *Male*	1	6
Irish Heroine. A Drama in 5 Acts. By Rev. J. de Concilio (*Mixed*)	1	6
Julia; or, The Gold Thimble. A Drama in One Act. By Mrs. J. Sadlier. *Female*	1	6
Knights of the Cross, The. A Sacred Drama in Three Acts. *Male*	2	6
Laurence and Xystus; or, the Illustrious Roman Martyrs. A Sacred Drama in Five Acts. *Male*	2	6
Major John Andre. An Historical Drama, Five Acts. *Male*	3	0
Marie Antoinette. An Historical Drama. *Female*	2	6
St. Helena; or, the Finding of the Holy Cross. A Drama in Three Acts. By Rev. J. A. Bergrath. *Female*	1	6
St. Louis in Chains. Drama, Five Acts. *Male*	3	0
Sylvia, and other Dramas.	6	0

All these prices are *nett.* (no reduction).

For the convenience of purchasers the following books referred to in the previous pages are arranged according to price:

6d.

A Friendly Voice; or, the Daily Monitor.
The Brigand Chief, and other Tales
Now is the Accepted Time, &c.
What a Child can Do, and other Tales
Sowing Wild Oats, &c.
The Two Hosts, and other Tales
The Lost Children of Mount St. Bernard
The Baker's Boy; or, the Results of Industry
A Broken Chain

The Golden Thought of Queen Beryl; The Brother's Grave
The Rod that Bore Blossoms; Patience and Impatience
Clare's Sacrifice
Nellie Gordon, the Factory Girl
Sir Ælfric, and other Tales
Adolphus; or, the Good Son
Nicholas; or, the Reward of a Good Action
Pope Pius IX. By White
Our Blessed Lady of Lourdes
Various Dramas (see page 19)

1s.

Father Placid
Rose Fortescue
Moothoosawmy and other Indian Tales, by Lady Herbert
Emily, Nancy, &c., by Lady Herbert
Two Cousins, &c., by Lady Herbert
Kainer; or, the Usurer's Doom
The Fairy Ching
The Two Friends
Yellow Holly, and other Tales
Tableaux Vivants, and other Tales
Wet Days, and other Tales
Fatal Consequence of Telling Lies
Tom's Crucifix, and Pat's Rosary
Good for Evil, and Joe Ryan's Repentance
The Old Prayer Book, and Charlie Pearson's Medal
Stories for my Children

Life of St. Benedict
Catherine's Promise, and Norah's Temptation
Annie's First Prayer, and Only a Picture
St. Patrick
My Dream and other Verses.
St. Bridget and other Saints of Ireland
Bertram Eldon
Story of a Paper Knife
The Village Lily
The Angels and the Sacraments
Sir Ælfric and other Tales
Diary of a Confessor of the Faith
Life, Passion, Death, and Resurrection of Our Lord
St. Edmund of Canterbury
Our Lady of Lourdes
The Ever Blessed Virgin

Little Books of St. Nicholas. Tales for Children. By Rev. Francis Drew. 1s. each. Nos. 1 to 8 are ready.

1. Oremus; 2. Dominus Vobiscum; 3. Pater Noster; 4. Per Jesum Christum; 5. Veni Creator; 6. Credo; 7. Ave Maria; 8. Ora pro nobis; 9. Corpus Christi; 10. Dei Genitrix; 11. Requiem; 12. Miserere; 13. Deo Gratias; 14. Guardian Angel.

1s. 6d.

Agnes Wilmott's History
The Golden Thought and other Tales
A Daughter of S. Dominic
Legends of the XIIIth Century.
Sketches of Life in Iceland
Paul Seigneret
Flowers of Christian Wisdom

Fairy Tales for Little Children
The Memoirs of a French Child
Walter Ferrers' School Days
Sir Thomas Maxwell and his Ward
The Mission Cross
Catherine Hamilton

2s.

Life of St. Mildred
The Adventures of a Protestant in Search of a Religion
Life of St. Benedict
To Rome and Back
Life of St. Wenefred
A Month at Lourdes
The Three Wishes
Terry O'Flinn

Twelve Stories of the Jewish Church
The Monk of the Monastery of Yuste (Charles V.)
Catherine Grown Older
Countess Adelstan
Story of the Life of St. Paul
Recollections of Card. Wiseman

2s. 6d.

Bobbie and Birdie
Our Esther
Gamekeeper's Little Son
My Golden Days
Little Rose of the Sacred Heart
Cassilda; or, the Moorish Princess of Toledo
Captain Rougemont; or, the Miraculous Conversion
Bertha; or the Consequences of a Fault
Father Mathew
Anthony; or, the Silver Crucifix
The Better Part
Blanche de Marsil'y
The Burgomaster's Daughter
Indian Sketches
George Lawson

Instructions for First Communicants
Great-Grandmother's Secret
Marcelle
Tales
The Story of Marie, and other
The Adventures of a Casket
Life of St. Mary Magdalene
The Orphan of Alsace
Life of St. Philomena
The Priest of Auvrigny
Strange Village and other Stories
The Village Steeple
The Battle of Connemara
Industry and Laziness
Sophia and Eulalie—Catholic Pilgrim's Progress
Holy Places

3s.

The Most Beautiful among the Children of Men
For Better, *not* For Worse
True Wayside Tales
Gathered Gems from Spanish Authors
Gretchen's Gift
Cistercian Legends
Chats about the Commandments
Chats about the Rosary
Margarethe Verflassen

The Conquest of Grenada
Out in the Cold World
Jack's Boy
The Feasts of Camelot
Fluffy : a Tale for Boys
Catherine Hamilton & Catherine grown Oldes
Pearl among the Virtues
Barbara Leigh   The Lost Son
St. Angela Merici

3s. 6d.

Tales from many Lands
Tim O'Halloran's Choice
Tom's Crucifix, and other Tales
The Adventures of a Protestant in Search of a Religion
My Lady at Last
The Rose of Venice
St. Francis of Assisi
Stories of Martyr Priests
Legends of the Saints
Father Benvenuto Bambozzi
Eagle and Dove

Stories of the Saints. 1st Series
Stories of the Saints. 2nd Series
Stories of the Saints. 3rd Series
Stories of the Saints. 4th Series
Stories of the Saints. 5th Series
Stories of Holy Lives
Blessed Giovanni Colombini
Gregory Lopez, the Hermit
Ven. Canori Mora
Venerable Anna Maria Taigi
Life of Fr. Hermann
Rest, on the Cross

4s.

Maidens of Hallowed Names
Adventures of a Casquet
My First Communion
Fisherman's Daughter. By Munroe
Great Grandmother's Secret
Paradise of God
Bertha ; or, the Consequence of a Fault
Dalaraida ; or, the Days of King Milcho
Conscience's, The Amulet
The Young Doctor
The Fisherman's Daughter
Count Hugo
The Conscript and Blind Rosa
The Village Innkeeper

Happiness of Being Rich
Ludovic and Gertrude
The Truce of God
Memoirs of a Guardian Angel
Adventures of a Captain
Fickle Fortune
The Four Seasons
Golden Sands. 1st Series
Golden Sands. 2nd Series
The King's Page and other Stories
Marcelle. A true story
Only a Waif
Souvenir of the Novitiate
Vacation Days
History of the Italian Revolution

R. Washbourne's Catalogue.

5s.

St. Vincent Ferrer
St. Bernardine of Siena
St. Philip Benizi
St. Veronica Giuliani
St. John of God
Recollections of a Missionary
The Days of King Milcho
Only a Waif

Butler's Lives of the Saints, selected by Mgr. Goddard
Killed at Sedan
Alice Harmon and other Tales
Bible History. Illustrated
The Joint Venture
Catholic Keepsake

6s.

Lives of the Early Popes
Albertus Magnus
Life of Mother Mary Jacqueline Favre, and others
Life of Sister Claude Simplicienne Fardel, and others
St. Columba
St. Boniface
Perico the Sad and other Tales
Panegyrics of Father Segneri
The Knowledge of Mary
The O'Mahony
Raphaela

Six Sunny Months and other Stories
Stray Leaves and other Stories
Thalia. An Historical Tale
The Two Brides
Alba's Dream and other Stories
Assunta Howard and other Stories
Emerald Gems
Letters of a Young Irishwoman to her Sister
Louise Lateau

6s. 6d., to 48s.

Life of Père Hermann, 4s. 6d.
Père Lacordaire, 6s. 6d.
Life of St. Francis Xavier, 8s.
Goffine's Explanation of the Epistles and Gospels. Illustrated. 9s.
Lives of First Religious of the Visitation. 2 vols., 10s.
Life of St. Ligouri, 10s.
Life of the Blessed Virgin. Illustrated. 10s.
Genius of Christianity. 10s. 6d.
True Men as we need them. 10s. 6d.
Louisa Kirkbride. 10s. 6d.

Lives of Irish Martyrs and Confessors. 12s.
Spalding's Reformation, 14s.
Pictorial Lives of the Saints. 15s.
Butler's Lives of the Saints. 2 vols., 28s., gilt, 36s.
St. Jure's Knowledge and Love of Our Lord. 3 vols., 31s. 6d.
Butler's Lives of the Saints. 4 vols., 36s., gilt, 42s.
Cardinal Wiseman's Essays. 6 vols., 36s.
Darras' Church History. 4 vols. 48s.

HOLY FAMILY CARD OF MEMBERSHIP.

A BEAUTIFUL DESIGN : All who have seen it admire it, and say Nothing equals it.

Price 6d., or post free, on a roller, 8d. Twelve copies 4s. 6d., or 5s. post free.

Medals, 3d., 4d., and 6d. each.

FIRST COMMUNION CARD.

This is also a very Beautiful Design, and commends itself to all who have seen it. It is also arranged as a Memento of Confirmation and Baptism.

Price 6d., or post free, on a roller, 8d. Twelve copies for 4s. 6d., or post free 5s.

Medals in Silver, 1s., 2s., and 3s. 6d. each.

CHILDREN OF MARY CARD.

Price 9d., or post free, on a roller, 1s.

Medals, 2d. and 3d. each ; or in Silver, 1s., 1s. 6d., 2s., 3s., 4s., 5s., 6s. 6d., and 10s. 6d. each.

Child of Mary Manual, 1s. Rule, 1d.

R. Washbourne's COMPLETE Catalogue, post free.

THE CHILD'S PICTURE PRAYER BOOK.

In simple language and in large type, on good paper, beautifully Illustrated.

The Contents of the book are Morning Prayers, The Angelus, Grace before and after Meals, Night Prayers, Litany of the Blessed Virgin, The Memorare, Prayers during Holy Mass, Divine Praises, Benediction of the Most Blessed Sacrament, Hymns, De Profundis, and the Rosary for the Dead.

The illustrations are 16 in number, each occupying a full page.

The binding is in cloth, with a cover designed expressly for the book and the price, with the pictures in two tints, is 1s., or in prettier binding, 1s. 6d.; full gilt, 2s.; with the pictures in seven colours, 1s. 6d., or in prettier binding, 2s.; full gilt, 2s. 6d.

THE LITTLE GARDEN ILLUSTRATED.

Abridged in the Latin, with 16 full-page Illustrations: cloth, 1s., with Epistles and Gospels, 1s. 6d.; roan, 1s. 6d.; French morocco, 2s. ditto, extra gilt, 2s. 6d.; calf or morocco, 3s. 6d.; ditto, extra gilt, 4s. 6d.; with Epistles and Gospels 6d. extra on the above.

R. WASHBOURNE'S POPULAR EDITION
OF
THE GARDEN OF THE SOUL.

This edition of THE GARDEN OF THE SOUL is especially distinguished by bearing the IMPRIMATUR OF THE CARDINAL-ARCHBISHOP OF WESTMINSTER. Amongst the many valuable additions, not before inserted in THE GARDEN OF THE SOUL, will be found the rites of administering the Sacraments in Latin and English, Devotions to the Sacred Heart, Devotion of the Quarant 'Ore, the Prayers for a Journey, or Itinerarium, Devotions to the Angel Guardians, The Way of the Cross, the Devotion of the Bona Mors, and many other devotions, and the Vespers in ordinary use. Especial attention is directed to the excellent paper and bold type used in the edition.

Embossed, 1s.; with rims and clasps, 1s. 6d.; with Epistles and Gospels 1s. 6d.; with rims and clasp, 2s. French morocco, 2s.; with rims and clasps, 2s. 6d.; with Epistles and Gospels, 2s. 6d.; with rims and clasps, 3s. French morocco, extra gilt, 2s. 6d.; with rims and clasp, 3s.; with Epistles and Gospels, 3s.; with rims and clasp, 3s. 6d.

Calf or morocco, 4s., with clasp, 5s. 6d.; extra gilt, 5s., or 6s. 6d. with clasp. Calf or morocco, extra gilt, 5s., with clasp, 6s. 6d. Morocco with two patent clasps, 12s. Morocco antique, with corners and two clasps, 18s. Velvet, with rims and clasp, 8s., 10s. 6d., 13s. Russia, with clasp, 10s., 12s. 6d. Russia antique, with corners and two clasps, 20s. Ivory, with rims and clasp, 12s. 6d., 16s., 20s., 22s. 6d.

Any of the above can be had with Epistles and Gospels, 6d. extra The Epistles and Gospels may be had separately, cloth, 6d., or 4s. per dozen; roan, 1s. 6d.

www.ingramcontent.com/pod-product-compliance
Lightning Source LLC
Chambersburg PA
CBHW022147160426
43197CB00009B/1460